# Short
# Dictionary of
# Classical Word Origins

# MIDCENTURY -
# REFERENCE LIBRARY

## DAGOBERT D. RUNES, Ph.D., *General Editor*

## AVAILABLE

Beethoven Encyclopedia
Dictionary of American Grammar
and Usage
Dictionary of the American Language
Dictionary of American Literature
Dictionary of American Maxims
Dictionary of American Proverbs
Dictionary of American Synonyms
Dictionary of Ancient History
Dictionary of Anthropology
Dictionary of Arts and Crafts
Dictionary of the Arts
Dictionary of Civics and Government
Dictionary of Dietetics
Dictionary of Early English
Dictionary of Etiquette
Dictionary of European History
Dictionary of Foreign Words
and Phrases
Dictionary of Last Words
Dictionary of Latin Literature
Dictionary of Linguistics
Dictionary of Magic
Dictionary of Mysticism
Dictionary of Mythology
Dictionary of New Words
Dictionary of Pastoral Psychology
Dictionary of Philosophy

Dictionary of Psychoanalysis
Dictionary of Russian Literature
Dictionary of Science and Technology
Dictionary of Sociology
Dictionary of Spanish Literature
Dictionary of Word Origins
Dictionary of World Literature
Encyclopedia of Aberrations
Encyclopedia of the Arts
Encyclopedia of Atomic Energy
Encyclopedia of Criminology
Encyclopedia of Literature
Encyclopedia of Psychology
Encyclopedia of Religion
Encyclopedia of Substitutes and
Synthetics
Encyclopedia of Vocational Guidance
Illustrated Technical Dictionary
Labor Dictionary
Liberal Arts Dictionary
Military and Naval Dictionary
New Dictionary of American History
New Dictionary of Psychology
Protestant Dictionary
Slavonic Encyclopedia
Theatre Dictionary
Tobacco Dictionary
Yoga Dictionary

## FORTHCOMING

Buddhist Dictionary
Dictionary of American Folklore
Dictionary of the American Indian
Dictionary of American Men and Places
Dictionary of American Names
Dictionary of American Superstitions
Dictionary of Astronomy
Dictionary of Discoveries and Inventions
Dictionary of Earth Sciences
Dictionary of Explorations
Dictionary of French Literature
Dictionary of Geography

Dictionary of German Literature
Dictionary of Hebrew Literature
Dictionary of Law
Dictionary of Mechanics
Dictionary of Poetics
Dictionary of the Renaissance
Dictionary of Science
Dictionary of Social Science
Encyclopedia of Morals
Personnel Dictionary
Teachers' Dictionary
Writers' Dictionary

## PHILOSOPHICAL LIBRARY, INC.
### Publishers

15 E. 40th Street                    New York 16, N. Y.

# Short
# Dictionary of
# Classical Word Origins

by

*Harry E. Wedeck*

*Lecturer in Classics, Brooklyn College, New York*

PHILOSOPHICAL LIBRARY

NEW YORK

# *Foreword*

This dictionary embraces the lexicographical field of words, phrases, and allusions that stem from classical sources or in some historical, literary, scientific, semantic, or philosophical implication are associated with classical culture. In an encyclopedic sense, the material ranges from Aristotelian catharsis to the Wooden Horse of Troy, from Homeric epic techniques to semantic distinctions in contemporary vocabulary. It discusses informally, concisely, schisms and sacred animals, the Atomic Theory and eclecticism, palinodes and libations and other features that occur with varying frequency in connection with a study or an interest in the classical tradition, in its most wide-ranging sense.

Although the book is not intended to be exhaustive, it does deal with the more significant items, or with items that, although more rare in popular contexts, have a value for their traditional association or their own status and impact in the history of human thought and expression.

H. E. W.

# *Introductory*

In the title of this book, the most important element is *Classical*, with a capital *C*, for here the term refers to the *Classics* or principal literary works of Ancient Greece and Ancient Rome. Both the noun *Classic* and the adjective *Classical* have gained a place in the language of every day, for do we not speak of something forming 'a *classical*, or *classic*, example' of so-and-so, and of something else, even if it's nothing more epoch-making than a horse race, being 'a *classic*'? 'A *classic(al)* example' derives from the vocabulary of the literary critics and grammarians and historians of Ancient Rome: *locus classicus*, literally 'a classical place,' so named because it occurs in a Classic, hence 'a classical passage'—the passage that best exemplifies, for instance, a certain usage. And 'a *classic*' is a sort of shorthand for 'a Classic, or Classical, author or book or poem or what have you,' therefore an excellent one. We now can go so far as to use such a phrase as 'a *classic* occasion,' where *classic* bears the sense 'memorable' or 'distinguished.'

Whether we read such grave and formidable subjects as philosophy, science, the higher-browed criticism of books, music, art, theatre, cinema; or whether we feel that we've done enough for culture and ourselves by reading such middle-brow matter as history, biography and autobiography; or whether we think we're proving ourselves to be serious, perhaps weighty, characters by indulging in short stories (preferably, of course, in a magazine) and, if it happens to be a wet evening or there's nothing especially good on radio or TV, by adventuring into a full-length novel; or, finally, whether the extent of our reading is sternly confined to the pages of a newspaper or even—refuse to believe it, if you're the rash, brash kind of person—of a 'comic' or 'funny':—whatever we read, and whether we're morons or geniuses, we are constantly, indeed on every page and probably in every paragraph, being brought up against a reference to Greek or Roman history or mythology or literature. Those references and allusions are inevitably expressed in words and phrases of either Greek or Latin origin, or, as so often happens, of both Greek and Latin origin; numerous Greek words and phrases, and allusions too, have passed through the intermediaries of Roman thought and Latin wording.

Nearly all these words, phrases, allusions—and, heaven knows, there are hundreds, there are thousands of them—are readily understood only if we know their origins; without exception, all of them are fully understood only if we truly know, not merely guess at, their origins.

But not more than .5% of the population of the U.S.A. and of the British Commonwealth of Nations could be accused of knowing any Ancient Greek; and not more than 5% (a fulsomely flattering figure) any Latin. So what are all the others going to do about it? Most of them, complacent in their ignorance, won't do anything; after all, what they don't miss won't help them.

Those who wish to do something about overcoming the very severe handicap—so very much severer than they suspect—of having 'small Latin, and less Greek' can do one of two things.

The first way is, to use a good general dictionary, such as *The American College Dictionary* or *Webster's Collegiate Dictionary* or *Webster's New World Dictionary* (amazingly good for etymologies or word-origins), or, if you want something bigger, *Webster's New International Dictionary* or *Wyld's Universal English Dictionary* or *The Shorter Oxford Dictionary*, all three excellent for word-histories. This way, although adequate for the majority of inquiries, is yet to be adjudged a second-best.

The second and better way is to use a dictionary that deals specifically with words and phrases of Classical origin and, at the same time, with references and especially with allusions to the history and the mythology, the literature and the philosophy, and also to the science and technology of Ancient Greece and Ancient Rome. We must never forget that the Greeks always 'had a word for it, but equally we must never forget that, in the arts, and the art, of civilization, they usually had also a way for it. Less philosophical and subtle than the Greeks, the Romans far less often supply the word; in the practical things of life, for instance in engineering of all kinds, they more often had the way of it.

But why have I said 'a dictionary'?—as if there existed a number of such specific dictionaries, and all I needed to do was to name the best of them! Off-hand, the only one I can think of is this *Dictionary of Classical Word Origins*, written—not merely compiled—by Dr. Harry E. Wedeck, well-known for his work in Classical studies. But even that statement is unfair, both to this book and to its author. Dr. Wedeck's dictionary performs honourably a task that badly needed doing. By 'honourably' I mean that although a few well-read persons will be able to inveigh self-righteously against this or that omission, the omissions are far fewer than the persons; also that, although certain persons may take exception to this, that or the other definition or interpretation, these persons will be hypercritics.

*A Dictionary of Classical Word Origins* possesses the great merit of insidious persuasion. Once you start using it, you will begin to dip here and there; once you start dipping, you'll begin to read consecutive entries or pages; once you start reading, as opposed to consulting, you will go on reading. More than that: you have but to pick up this book and you'll 'start something'—something you will later be glad you *did* start.

When you've read this dictionary, you'll no longer have trouble with, and no longer feel embarrassed at your horrible and disgusting ignorance of, such tricky matters and important, yet hitherto mysterious, events or ideas as are embedded in the numerous strata of the Greek and Ancient World. No longer will you be impaled upon *the horns of a dilemma;* fail to untie a *Gordian knot,* a feat rather melodramatically performed by Alexander of Macedon, Alexander the Great, Alexander the demigod; be unable to *cross the Rubicon;* fear the *Ides of March;* feel cheated by a *Pyrrhic victory;* wonder when *at the Greek Kalends* (compare our *calendar*) could be; and dread the thought of having, one day, to *cross the Styx.* You will be able to enjoy *Homeric laughter* and a *Roman holiday* and mingle with the *jovial,* the *mercurial* and the *saturnine;* to appreciate a *Junoesque* woman and a 'pocket *Hercules*'; to avoid the wiles of a *Circe* and, not too distantly, admire the charms of a *Venus,* especially if, on the one hand, you're an *Apollo* or, on the other, a *Nestor* or a *Mentor;* to share the intellectual delights of a *Socratic argument* (or *dialogue*) or an *Aristotelian* handbook to knowledge, 'the *eloquence of Demosthenes*' no less than 'a *Ciceronian* style.' These and many other things will you learn and, by learning, have come to understand and therefore to enjoy, by a leisurely and surprisingly pleasant reading of this *Dictionary of Classical Word Origins.*

ERIC PARTRIDGE

# A

**Abdera:** This city, at the Northern part of the Aegean Sea, was proverbially associated with stupidity, although at least two famous Greeks were born there: Protagoras and Democritus.

**Aberrant:** Straying: deviating. From two Latin words meaning *wandering away*.

**Ability in Mathematics Required:** This statement, emphasizing the importance of mathematical study, was inscribed over the door of Plato's Academy.

**Abnegation:** Renunciation: denial. From a Latin word meaning *to deny*.

**Aborigines:** Primitive races, indigenous to a country. From two Latin words meaning *from the beginning*.

**Academy:** An institution of learning. The expression is derived from the Academy, an Athenian garden grove where the Greek philosopher Plato established the first university.

**Achates:** The faithful companion of the Trojan hero Aeneas. In Latin, he is called fidus Achates—devoted Achates. The expression is now used in an analogous sense: for instance, James Boswell was the fidus Achates of Dr. Johnson, as Dr. Watson was of Sherlock Holmes.

**Acheron:** According to ancient mythology, a river in Hades.

**Achilles' heel:** Symbolically, this expression means a vulnerable spot. Thetis, Achilles' mother, according to Greek mythology, held her son by the heel when she dipped him into the River Styx to make him invulnerable in the Trojan War. His heel, however, was untouched by the protective water.

**Achromatic:** Colorless. From two Greek words meaning *no color*.

**Acoustics:** Conditions of hearing. From a Greek word meaning *to hear*.

**Acrimonious:** Caustic: ill-tempered. From a Latin word meaning *sharp*.

**Acrophobia:** A fear of heights. From two Greek words meaning *fear of high places*.

**Acropolis:** In Athens, a fortified hill summit crowned by the Parthenon and other temples and by statues. From two Greek words meaning *a high city*.

**Actor Primarum:** The Latin term for a leading man in a theatrical performance.

**Adamant:** Used in an adjectival sense, as it usually is, it means stubborn. From two Greek words meaning *not subdued*.

**Adherent:** A disciple: a follower. From a Latin word meaning *clinging*.

**Adoxography:** Writing cleverly on a low or trifling theme. From two Greek words meaning *inglorious writing*.

**Aegis:** Protection: sponsorship: auspices. In Greek mythology, the aegis was the emblem of Zeus. In later mythology, it was represented as a goatskin hanging over the shoulders of Athena.

**Aeolian:** In ancient mythology, Aeolus was king of the winds. Aeolian melodies are such as are caused by the breezes. Dust and sand carried by winds from one area to another form what are called aeolian deposits.

**Aeon:** An infinite age: an indeterminate period. From a Greek word meaning *a period of time*.

**Aesthetic:** Relating to what is beautiful: appreciative of beauty. From a Greek word meaning *to feel, to perceive*.

**Affidavit:** Testimony written under oath. From a Latin word meaning *to state on oath*.

**Agape:** In early Christianity, the agape was a meeting of Christian members. In Greek agape means *love*.

**Agelast:** A person who never laughs. From a Greek word meaning *not laughing*.

**Agenda:** A program of business: matters proposed for discussion or action. From a Latin word meaning *things that must be done*.

**Agon:** In Greek comedy, a debate between two characters, as in the comedies of Aristophanes. Agon itself means in Greek *a contest* or *debate*.

**Agora:** In ancient Greek cities, particularly in Athens, a market place: a place of assembly, where men met for intellectual or social talk, lectures, and discussion. The Greek word agora means *a market place;* originally, *an assembly*.

**Agrarian:** Associated with agriculture, fields, land. From a Latin word meaning *field*. Agrarian Laws are enactments regulating the distribution and management of public lands.

**Aidos:** A Greek word, used in Homer, meaning a *sense of shame* or *honor* that prevented a person from breaking the unwritten tribal laws.

**Alexandria:** In addition to the first city so named, in the fourth century B.C., in Egypt, numerous other cities, both in ancient and in modern times, have assumed the name that stems from the eponym Alexander the Great.

**All is flux:** This is a translation of the Greek *Panta rei,* the doctrine of the Greek philosopher Heraclitus, who envisaged the evolutionary process.

**Allopathic:** Relating to remedies that produce effects different from the effects of the disease. From two Greek words meaning *other suffering*.

**Alma Mater:** A Latin phrase meaning *fostering mother:* applied to an institution at which a person has been a student.

**Alpha and Omega:** The beginning and the end, the entirety. Alpha is the first letter, and omega the last letter, in the Greek alphabet.

**Alphabet:** This is the Anglicized form of the first two letters of the Greek alphabet: alpha, beta. The early Greek alphabet stems from a Phoenician source.

**Altruism:** Concern for others: unselfishness. From a Latin word meaning *other*.

**Amanuensis:** A secretary: a scribe. From a Latin word meaning *hand*.

**Amazon:** A muscular, belligerent woman. The expression possibly stems from two Greek words meaning *breastless*. The Amazons were women whose empire extended along the shores of the Black Sea. Their custom was to cut off the right breast, in female children, for ease in later practice with bow and arrow. Under their queen Penthesilea, the Amazons fought, in the Trojan War, as allies of the Trojans against the Greeks.

**Ambidextrous:** Skilled with both hands. In a pejorative sense, double-dealing. From two Latin words meaning *both right hands*.

**Ambiguous:** Doubtful, uncertain. From two Latin words meaning *driving around*.

**Ambrosia:** A substance consumed by the ancient gods as food. It is mentioned in the Homeric poems. From Greek words meaning *immortal*.

**Amphibian:** Relating to both land and sea: a creature able to live on land and sea. From two Greek words meaning *both lives*.

**Amphictionies:** In Greek history, leagues associated with the observance of religious cults in temples. From two Greek words meaning *those who live round about*.

**Amulets:** A charm, talisman, periapt: used for apotropaic purposes. From a Latin word meaning *a charm*. In ancient Greece and Italy charms were considered as potent means of thwarting maleficent operations due to witchcraft or of endowing the possessor with magic virtues.

**Anachronism:** A mistake in time, that misplaces events: an antedating of a fact or an event. From two Greek words meaning *backward in time*.

**Anacreontic:** Erotic, convivial. The expression is associated with love and wine. Anacreon was a Greek lyric poet whose themes were wine, women and song.

**Anagnorisis:** This Greek word means *discovery,* or *recognition:* a change from ignorance to knowledge, love to hate, or sometimes from hate to love. The expression belongs in Aristotelian dramatic criticism, and applies to the techniques of Greek tragic drama.

**Analogy:** A relationship: a similarity: a resemblance. From a Greek expression meaning *proportionate.*

**Anarchy:** A state without rule: political chaos: disorder. From two Greek words meaning *no rule.*

**Anathema:** A curse: a person or thing accursed: an object of intense repulsion. From a Greek word meaning *devoted, dedicated.*

**Ancillary:** Subordinate, auxiliary. From a Latin word meaning *a maidservant.*

**Androgynous:** Having male and female characteristics. Synonymous with hermaphroditic. From two Greek words meaning *man* and *woman.*

**Annihilation:** The act of reducing to nothing: the condition of nothingness. From a Latin word meaning *nothing.*

**Anodyne:** A means of freeing from pain. From two Greek words meaning *no pain.*

**Anomaly:** An irregularity: an exception. From two Greek words meaning *irregular.*

**Anonymous:** Nameless: without a known name. From two Greek words meaning *without a name.*

**Antagonist:** One who contends with another: an opponent. The expression stems from two Greek words meaning *an adversary, a combatant.*

**Anthology:** A collection of distinctive passages in prose or verse. From a Greek word meaning *a bouquet.*

**Anthropocentric:** Relating to man as the central fact in nature. From two Greek words meaning *man in the centre.*

**Antistrophe:** In Greek dramatic poetry, part of a choral lyric in which only half of the chorus participates.

**Antithesis:** A contrast, expressed by contrasting words. From two Greek words meaning *setting against*.

**Antonym:** A word of opposite meaning. From two Greek words meaning *one word instead of* (another).

**Apiary:** A place for bees: a collection of bee hives. From two Latin words meaning *a place for bees*.

**Apocalypse:** Revelation. From two Greek words meaning *to uncover*.

**Apocryphal:** Spurious: not authentic: of doubtful authorship. From two Greek words meaning *hiding away*.

**Apologue:** A fable containing a moral lesson: an allegory. From two Greek words meaning *from a speech*.

**Apogee:** Culmination: height. From a Greek word meaning *the point at which a heavenly body is farthest away from the earth*. The antonym of apogee is perigee, meaning the *depths, the lowest point*.

**Apostate:** One who renounces his religious faith, as Julian the Apostate: a renegade. From two Greek words meaning *standing away*.

**Apothegm:** A pithy saying: a maxim. From a Greek word meaning *something spoken*.

**Apotropaic:** Intended to avert. From two Greek words meaning *turning aside*.

**Apple of Discord:** A cause for a dispute. In Greek mythology, at a banquet of the gods, Discord threw down an apple 'for the fairest.' The resultant beauty contest, in which Juno, Minerva, and Venus participated, precipitated the Trojan War.

**Aquarium:** A place where fish are kept: a place for aquatic plants or animals. From two Latin words meaning *a place for water*.

**Aqueducts:** One of the major Roman structural achievements, of which remains are still to be found in France and Spain.

From two Latin words meaning *conducting water*. A textbook on the subject, by Frontinus, who flourished in the first century A.D., is extant.

**Arachnid:** In biology, a scientific term for spider. In Greek mythology, Arachne was a princess who was changed into a spider.

**Arbiter:** A judge: a critic. From a Latin word meaning *a judge*. Among the Romans, the arbiter elegantiarum was a kind of master of ceremonies who presided over banquets and supervised the drinking by the guests. The most famous arbiter elegantiarum in literary history was Petronius, author of the Satyricon.

**Arcadian:** Pastoral, bucolic, untroubled. Arcadia was a mountainous, pastoral region in the Peloponnesus of Greece.

**Archaeology:** The study of antiquity, of past cultures. From two Greek words meaning the *study of what is ancient*.

**Archaism:** An obsolete expression: an antiquated form. From a Greek word meaning *old*.

**Archetype:** Original pattern: model. From a Greek word meaning *first pattern*.

**Architectonic:** Architectural: structural. The architectonics of a speech means its rhetorical and logical construction. From two Greek words meaning *a chief* or *master builder*.

**Archytas:** A Pythagorean philosopher of the fourth century B.C. who invented a wooden dove that could fly.

**Arena:** This word, now used of a sporting, athletic area, derives from the Latin word arena, meaning *sand*. Sand was sprinkled in the Roman Colosseum to absorb the gladiators' and animal blood spilt during combats.

**Areopagus:** An Athenian Council that had certain juridical functions and that convened on the Areopagus hill.

**Arete:** A Greek word used in philosophical contexts, meaning *virtue* or *excellence*.

**Argonauts:** Pioneers, adventurers. In Greek mythology, the Argonauts were a band of heroes who, under the leadership of Jason, sailed in search of the Golden Fleece. The word means *sailors in the ship Argo*.

**Argus-eyed:** Applied to a person who is extremely observant. In Greek mythology, Argus was a creature who possessed one hundred eyes.

**Aristocracy:** This word is a combination of two words of Greek origin meaning *the rule of the best:* that is, the best in regard to birth.

**Artifact:** An object of art or of human skill, such as a primitive mask or vessel. From two Latin words meaning *made by skill*.

**Astrology:** The study of the stars as they affect human affairs by forecasting future events. From two Greek words meaning *the study of the stars*. A certain Firmicus Maternus wrote a Latin treatise on the subject. In the Middle Ages astrology was a widely popular study. The most significant work in the seventeenth century was J. B. Morin de Villefranche's Astrologia Gallica.

**Astronomy:** The study of the stars and the heavenly bodies. From two Greek words meaning *arrangement of the stars*.

**Artemision:** A gigantic temple of Artemis, at Ephesus, the centre of a widespread cult of this nature goddess.

**Artists of Dionysus:** This was the title given in ancient Greece to actors in dramatic presentations.

**Ascetic:** A person dedicated to self-denial, to severe self-discipline. From a Greek word meaning *to exercise*.

**Asclepiadai:** Greek priest-physicians whose practice was associated with Asclepius, the god of healing.

**Ataraxia:** A Greek word meaning *imperturbability*. This was the goal of Epicurean philosophy.

**Atavistic:** Relating to ancestors: having characteristics of remote ancestors. From a Latin word meaning *an ancestor*.

**Athenaeum:** A name often given to a library, a learned society, or a club. The expression is associated with the name of Athens, the most cultured city of ancient Greece. In the reign of the Emperor Hadrian, the Athenaeum in Rome was an institute devoted to recitals and lectures.

**Athens, the School of Hellas:** A statement made by Pericles in his Funeral Oration. This speech, that appears in the account of the Peloponnesian War by the fifth century B.C. Greek historian Thucydides, postulates the intellectual superiority of Athenian culture.

**Athletics:** From a Greek word meaning *to contend for a prize.* The Greeks considered human perfection as a harmony of the physical and the intellectual man. Hence athletes had a dominant but not predominant place in Greek training. Athletics included running, jumping, discus and spear throwing, wrestling, and boxing. Such training was normally continued into middle age, and even later. Athletic contests were associated with religious festivals, which were called Panhellenic because they embraced the entire Greek race.

**Atlas:** In classical mythology, Atlas was a god represented as supporting the world on his shoulders. In the Middle Ages, an atlas—a collection of maps—usually had as a frontispiece a figure of Atlas upholding the universe.

**Atomic Theory:** According to Aristotle, the inventor of the Atomic Theory was Leucippus, who flourished in the fifth century B.C. The Atomic Theory was incorporated into the metaphysical speculations of the third century B.C. Greek philosopher Epicurus and of the Roman epic poet Lucretius who flourished in the first century B.C.

**Atrabilious:** Melancholy: depressed. From two Latin words meaning *black bile,* which was at one time believed to condition the temperament.

**Attic:** Denoting excellence in intellectual or artistic pursuits. The expression stems from the peninsula of Attica, of which the chief city was Athens, the cultural centre of Greece.

**Augean Stables:** 'To cleanse the Augean stables' signifies to make a clean sweep. In ancient mythology, Hercules had the task of cleaning the stables of King Augeas, that had not been cleaned for thirty years.

**Augury:** An omen, a prognosticative portent: the act of forecasting the future. Among the Romans, the augur was a priest who foretold the future by observation of the flight of birds.

**Augustus:** The Roman Imperial title Augustus, which means *holy, sacrosanct,* was anciently used in a religious sense.

**Aurora:** Aurora was the Greek and Roman goddess of the dawn. Homer calls her 'rosy-fingered.' The multi-colored lights that appear in the sky in northern latitudes are called the Aurora Borealis, the Northern Dawn.

**Auspices:** Patronage, care, protection. From two Latin words meaning *divination by observation of birds.*

**Automatic:** Self-acting. From two Greek words meaning *self-moving.*

**Autonomous:** Independent. From two Greek words meaning *ruling over oneself.*

**Autonomy:** Self-government. From two Greek words meaning *self-rule.*

**Aviary:** A place or enclosure for birds. From two Latin words meaning *a place for birds.*

**Avid:** Eager. From a Latin word meaning *longing for.*

**Axiom:** A self-evident maxim: a generally accepted truth. From a Greek word meaning *worthy.*

# B

**Bacchanal:** A drunken reveler. The expression derives from Bacchus, the Greek and Roman wine-god.

**Bacchanalia:** Roman religious orgies, associated with Bacchus, that were marked by wild license. From a Latin word meaning Bacchus, the Greek and Roman wine-god.

**Bacchanalian:** Relating to wild drunken revelry. The expression stems from Bacchus, the Greek and Roman wine-god.

**Bacchante:** A female devotee of Bacchus, who participates in drunken orgiastic rites. The expression derives from Bacchus, the Greek and Roman wine-god.

**Bacchic:** Relating to wine-drinking. The expression stems from Bacchus, the Greek and Roman wine-god.

**Ballistics:** The science of the motion of missiles. From a Greek word meaning *to throw*.

**Balneology:** The study of bathing in natural mineral waters as a therapeutic measure. From a Latin word and a Greek word meaning *the study of bathing*.

**Banausic:** Trivial. From a Greek word meaning *mechanical*. Aristotle considers that all banausic activities are unworthy of a free man.

**Barbarian:** To the Greeks, Barbarian meant merely non-Hellenic.

**Basilica:** In ancient Rome, a type of building that was used for social gatherings and for conducting law cases. The word stems from a Greek term meaning *royal*. In the Middle Ages, many basilicae were converted into Christian churches.

**Battology:** Stammering. Herodotus, in the Persian Wars, mentions that a certain Battos was a stammerer.

**Beatific:** Blissful, blessed. From a Latin word meaning *blessed, happy*.

**Best, the Wisest, and the Justest Man:** This description is applied, in Plato's dialogue Phaedo, to the philosopher Socrates.

**Biannual:** Occurring twice a year. From two Latin words meaning *twice* and *a year*.

**Biennial:** Occurring once in two years. From two Latin words meaning *twice* and *a year*.

**Big book is a big evil:** A statement made by Callimachus, a Greek poet of the third century B.C.

**Bireme:** A ship equipped with two banks of oars. From two Latin words meaning *two sets of oars*.

**Boeotia:** This region in Greece was proverbially associated with stupidity.

**Bombinate:** To resound, to boom. From a Latin word meaning *to resound*.

**Book Burning:** The first recorded burning of books, in this case the burning of books by the Sophist philosopher Protagoras, occurred in Athens in 411 B.C.

**Boulé:** The assembly of the Athenians, established by Solon, and consisting of four hundred members. Enlarged to 500 by Cleisthenes.

**Brekekekex Koax Koax:** This is the onomatopeic refrain of the frog chorus in "The Frogs," a comedy by the Greek poet Aristophanes. Yale University has adopted this refrain as part of its college cheer.

**Bucolic:** Relating to the country: pastoral: rustic. From a Greek word meaning *a cowherd*.

**Bus boy:** The Romans had slaves whose sole function was to remove dishes at a banquet. They were known as analectae.

# C

**Cacophony:** Discordant sounds: a combination of non-harmonious sounds. From two Greek words meaning *bad sounds*.

**Caduceus:** A rod, adorned with wings, and with two serpents entwined. It was the wand of Mercury, symbolizing his power of inducing sleep. Milton calls it the 'opiate rod.' One of the attributes of Mercury was the power of healing. Hence the caduceus is now the emblem of physicians.

**Calligraphy:** Handwriting. From two Greek words meaning *beautiful writing*.

**Calumny:** Slander: a false accusation. From a Latin word meaning *to slander*.

**Candidate:** An applicant for office. In Rome the person who sought public office wore a white toga—toga candida, that implied the purity of his character and motives.

**Canon:** A criterion: a rule: a formally recognized catalogue of books or persons. From a Greek word meaning *a rule*.

**Cantores Euphorionis:** This Latin expression, which means *the songsters of Euphorion,* was used by Cicero to describe contemporary Roman poets who followed the Greek poet Euphorion and other Alexandrian poets—all characterized by great erudition and a proneness to obscure literary allusiveness.

**Caret:** A typographical mark indicating that an item in a context has been omitted and is now inserted. From a Latin word meaning *lacking*.

**Carpe diem:** A Latin expression from one of the Roman poet Horace's Odes. Literally, it means: *Gather (the enjoyment of) the day:* that is, live for today. This hedonistic concept is characteristic of Horace. The Elizabethan poet Robert Herrick, in his *Counsel to Girls,* expresses the same thought:

> Gather ye rose-buds while ye may.
> Old Time is still a-flying.

**Cassandra:** The daughter of King Priam of Troy, endowed by Apollo with the gift of prophecy, but doomed to be unheeded. *J'étais Cassandre,* by Madame Tabouis, a French publicist, implies the author's prophetic but disregarded warnings about Nazi aggression during World War II.

**Cataclysm:** Disaster. From two Greek words meaning *washing down, deluge*.

**Catacombs:** In ancient Rome, the catacombs were underground burial places associated with the early Christians. From two Greek words meaning *a hollow place*.

**Catalogue:** A list, usually in alphabetical order. From two Greek words meaning *counting down*.

**Category:** A class: a classification: a division. From a Greek expression meaning *to harangue publicly*.

**Catharsis:** In Aristotelian dramatic criticism, a catharsis is an emotional purification through fear and pity, induced by a supremely effective dramatic presentation.

**Cathedral:** A church containing the cathedra, the Latin term for a seat or throne, in a religious sense. An ex cathedra statement is a categorical assertion issuing from the seat or chair of a professor or similar authority.

**Caucasus:** Among the Greeks and the Romans, the Caucasus region symbolizes the uttermost confines of barbarism. Prometheus, for instance, was bound to a rock in the Caucasus for defying Zeus. In the Aeneid, Dido declares that Aeneas' heartlessness indicates that he must have been born among the shaggy cliffs in the Caucasus.

**Celibate:** A bachelor: an unmarried person. From a Latin word meaning *unmarried*.

**Cenobite:** A member of a religious community. From two Greek words meaning *common life*.

**Cenotaph:** A monument in memory of a person buried elsewhere. The expression stems from two Greek words meaning *an empty tomb*.

**Censor:** One who takes a census: a critic. From a Latin word meaning the official whose function, in ancient Rome, was to take the census of persons and property and to regulate public morality.

**Centaurs:** In ancient mythology, monsters of the forests and mountains whose upper part was of human form and whose lower part was equine.

**Cento:** A medley of verses, consisting of lines taken from existing poems and rearranged to produce a pseudo-neo-poem. From a Latin word meaning *a patchwork cloak*. The composition of centos was a popular pastime in the Middle Ages.

**Ceramics:** The study or art of making baked clay, pottery. From a Greek word meaning *pottery*.

**Cerberus:** The three-headed dog that guarded the entrance to the lower regions. 'To give a sop to Cerberus' means to appease someone with a gift.

**Ceres:** Goddess of agriculture. The word cereal is associated with her name. Her attribute was a cornucopia—a horn of plenty.

**Cerulean:** Azure: blue. From a Latin word meaning *dark blue.*

**Chaos:** Confusion, disorder. The Greek word chaos, which means *a yawning chasm,* was associated with Chaos, the most ancient of the gods.

**Chimaera:** In ancient mythology, a triple-shaped, fire-breathing monster of lion, serpent, and goat form, that was finally slain by Bellerophon. From a Greek word meaning *a she-goat.*

**Chimerical:** Fantastic, fanciful. (See: Chimaera)

**Chios:** A Greek island where, it was claimed, Homer was born.

**Choregus:** In Greek drama, the wealthy sponsor of a play.

**Chrestomathy:** A selection of passages: an anthology, usually of texts helpful in the study of language. From two Greek words meaning *useful learning.*

**Chria:** In ancient rhetoric, a series of variations of phrases to express a particular thought.

**Chryselephantine:** Made of gold and ivory. From two Greek words meaning *gold and ivory.* This term was often applied to statues.

**Chthonic:** Relating to the earth: earthy. The term derives from a Greek word meaning *earth.*

**Cicerone:** A guide. From Cicero, the Roman orator. His eloquence was figuratively transferred to the volubility of the professional guide.

**Circuitous:** Roundabout: indirect. From two Latin words meaning *going around.*

**Circus:** An area where public displays of various kinds are held, especially performances of animals. From the Latin circus, a building devoted to horse and chariot races and similar contests. The most famous circus was the Circus Maximus, whose popularity was greatest in the first century B.C.

**Clandestine:** Secret: furtive. From a Latin word meaning *secretly*.

**Claustrophobia:** Fear of enclosed places. From a Latin and a Greek word meaning *fear of a confined place*.

**Cleostratus:** A sixth century B.C. Greek who was one of the founders of Greek astronomy.

**Codex:** In ancient bookmaking, the codex was a collection of papyrus leaves fastened together in the form of a modern book.

**Coeval:** Of the same age: contemporary. From two Latin words meaning *together in age*.

**College:** This word, which means an institute of learning, comes from the Latin collegium, which originally was associated with priestly functions, temple meetings, and religious rites. The Latin term Collegium Opificum was a Trade Union—or what would have been in mediaeval days a guild —consisting of men of the same trade. Trade Unions were suppressed by Julius Caesar owing to their participation in political agitation. But in Imperial times the collegia began to flourish again.

Carpenters had a union called fabri tignarii. Dendrophori were firewood dealers. Clothing makers belonged to the centonarii. The navicularii were shipowners, while the merchants' union was the negotiatores.

There was an initiation fee, followed by a monthly tax. Members met in a hall called a schola. Membership usually ranged from one to three hundred. Benefits included a common burial place and benevolent distributions.

**Colossus:** A monstrous statue or figure. The word is associated with the gigantic statue of Apollo called the Colossus, at Rhodes. It was one of the seven wonders of the ancient world.

**Comedy:** Comedy, which means a light, amusing play or situation, derives from two Greek words signifying *a song of festivity*. Such songs were anciently part of the celebrations in honor of Dionysus, god of fertility, and were marked by obscene hilarities. These festal songs were the source of later comedies presented as theatrical performances.

**Comity:** Ease of manner: suavity. From a Latin word meaning *mild, courteous.*

**Concept:** An idea. From a Latin word meaning *to conceive.*

**Concomitant:** Conjoined: as a noun, an accompanying factor. From two Latin words meaning *accompanying.*

**Concupiscence:** Lust. From a Latin word meaning *to desire.*

**Confiscate:** To seize for public use: to appropriate as forfeit. From two Latin words meaning *putting into the treasury.*

**Conjecture:** To deduce: to infer. From two Latin words meaning *to throw together.*

**Contiguity:** Closeness: nearness: proximity. From a Latin word meaning *to touch.*

**Controversia:** A rhetorical exercise practiced in ancient Rome, consisting of a discussion on some imaginary legal situation.

**Contumely:** Contempt: scorn: disdain. From a Latin word meaning *insolent.*

**Corax:** The first Greek rhetorician, who flourished in the fifth century B.C.

**Corollary:** In logical and mathematical reasoning, a deduction: an inference: a conclusion. From a Latin word meaning *a little crown.*

**Coruscating:** Glittering: brilliant. From a Latin word meaning *to glitter.*

**Coryphaeus:** A leader of a philosophical school: a leader in any field. From a Greek word meaning *a leader of a chorus.*

**Cos:** A Greek island that was the home of Greek medical science. Hippocrates, the father of medicine, was born in Cos in the fifth century B.C.

**Cosmology:** The study of the universe. From two Greek words meaning *study of the universe*. The early pre-Socratic philosophers were actually cosmologists or, in the literal sense, physiologists.

**Criterion:** A standard. From a Greek word meaning *a judge*.

**Croesus:** An ancient king of Lydia in Asia Minor, who was so wealthy that his name has become synonymous with vast riches.

**Cromnyomancy:** Divination by means of onions. An ancient practice associated with sorcery. From two Greek words meaning *divination by onions*.

**Cryptic:** Obscure: hidden. From a Greek word meaning *hidden*.

**Culmination:** Consummation: climax: ultimate realization. From a Latin word meaning *a height, a summit*.

**Cupid:** The god of love, son of Venus and Jupiter, is represented as a winged child, equipped with bow and arrow. In Latin, he is also Amor—Love: and is identified with the Greek Eros.

**Cursory:** Hasty: superficial. From a Latin word meaning *running*.

**Cyclopean Land:** This expression, used by the dramatic poet Euripides, refers to Argolis in Greece, of which the chief city was Mycenae. The walls of Mycenae, it was said, resembled those built by the Cyclops in Tiryns.

**Cynics:** The Cynics were Greek philosophers whose ideals were physical endurance and self-reliance. They held that the only good is virtue: the only evil, vice. The term cynic is associated with a Greek word meaning *dog*, because, according to one explanation, the Cynics were captious and always snarling.

**Cynosure:** The focus of attraction. From two Greek words meaning, astronomically, *the dog's tail:* that is, the pole star. In navigation, the pole star was a focal point in steering.

# D

**Daedal:** Skilled, variegated. The epithet is often applied to colorful autumn landscapes. From Daedalus, who, in Greek mythology, invented the labyrinth and a contraption for flying by means of wings.

**Daimon:** The daimon, which in Greek means *spirit,* was the supernatural 'voice' or 'sign' that always guided Socrates in his ethical mission and neglect of which usually produced unpleasant results.

**Dark Ages:** An expression applied to a period in the intellectual history of Europe extending from the beginning of the sixth century A.D. to the end of the eleventh century.

**Decalogue:** The Ten Commandments. From two Greek words meaning *ten speeches.*

**Decennium:** A period of ten years. From two Latin words meaning *ten years.*

**Declamation:** A speech. From a Latin word meaning an oratorical composition, the subject being some historical theme or an imaginary legal problem.

**Defalcate:** To embezzle. From a Latin word meaning *to cut off.*

**Delphi:** This religious centre, where the oracle of Apollo was delivered, was situated almost in the centre of Greece and hence was considered the omphalos or navel of the universe.

**Delphic:** Oracular, prophetic. This term derives from Delphi, near Mt. Parnassus in Greece, where a famous temple of

Apollo stood. Here the oracle of the god uttered ambivalent prophecies.

**Demiourgoi:** A Greek word meaning those who work for the people, craftsmen. In Platonic philosophy, Demiourgos means the Creator.

**Democracy:** This term derives from two Greek words meaning *rule of the people:* that is, the supreme power in the hands of the people, in a collective sense.

**Deodand:** According to an English law, abolished in 1846, a horse that killed its keeper became deodand: i.e., forfeit to the king. The expression is an Anglicized form of two Latin words meaning *to be given to God.*

**Deontology:** The science that involves the rules, obligations, and duties of any function. From a Greek word meaning *necessity.*

**Depredation:** Plundering: despoiling. From a Latin word meaning *to plunder.*

**Dereliction:** Neglect: failure. From a Latin word meaning *leaving behind.*

**Derisive:** Contemptuous: scornful. From a Latin word meaning *to laugh.*

**Desultory:** Rambling: disconnected: discursive. From a Latin word meaning *to leap down.*

**Deus ex machina:** A Latin phrase meaning *the god from the machine.* This was a mechanical device, in Greek drama, in which a god, suspended from a crane, appeared on the stage at a dramatic moment. The phrase is regularly used to mean an unexpected stratagem for solving a difficulty.

**Deuteragonist:** In Greek drama, an actor of second importance. The word stems from two Greek expressions meaning *second actor.*

**De Verborum Significatu:** This is the Latin title, meaning *The Significance of Words,* of the first Latin lexicon ever written. The author was Verrius Flaccus, who flourished in the first century A.D.

**Dexterity:** Skill: expertness. From a Latin word meaning *right hand.*

**Dialectics:** The art of logical disputation: the art of sound reasoning. From two Greek words meaning *the art of language.*

**Diaphanous:** Transparent: clear. From two Greek words meaning *showing through.*

**Diatribe:** A violent harangue: an abusive attack. This expression, which stems from a Greek word innocuously meaning *a pastime,* has undergone a sharply pejorative transformation.

**Dice:** According to a fragmentary passage in the work of the dramatist Sophocles, the invention of dice was due to a certain Palamedes, who hopefully dedicated a set of dice at the altar of the goddess Fortune.

**Dichotomy:** A division—implying opposition and contradicdiction. From two Greek words meaning *cut in two.*

**Dictator:** Among the Romans a dictator was an extraordinary magistrate who held office, above the two consuls, for a short time, usually six months, in a political or military emergency. The office, established in 501 B.C., was abolished in 44 B.C. The modern English word has acquired a pejorative significance.

**Didactic:** Intended to teach. From a Greek word meaning *to teach.* Many Greek and Latin poems were didactic in purpose: for example Hesiod's "Works and Days," and Lucretius' "The Nature of Things."

**Didoes:** 'To cut up didoes' means to play tricks, pranks. Dido, queen of Carthage, in Vergil's epic poem the Aeneid, cut up strips of hide to cover the widest possible extent of land for her new realms. This is a possible source of the English expression.

**Digital:** Relating to the fingers. From a Latin word meaning *finger.*

**Dilatory:** Tardy: slow: procrastinating. From a Latin word meaning *to defer, delay*.

**Diogenes:** An ancient Greek philosopher who was reputed to carry a lighted lamp, even by day, in search of an ideal honest man.

**Diomus:** A Sicilian cowherd, according to ancient legend, who sang the first bucolic poem.

**Diopter:** An instrument invented by Hipparchus for levelling and taking altitudes. From two Greek words meaning *to see through*.

**Diptych:** A picture in two contiguous parts: a two-leaved tablet. From two Greek words meaning *two fold*.

**Disciple:** A learner: a follower, often in a religious sense: an adherent of a person or a doctrine, in any sense. From a Latin word meaning *to learn*.

**Disparate:** Divergent: dissimilar. From two Latin words meaning *prepared separately* or *unequally*.

**Distich:** A couplet: two lines of verse. From a Greek word meaning *two verses*.

**Dithyramb:** A choral lyric in honor of Dionysus. The performers were men who, dressed in goatskins, represented satyrs, the attendants of the god.

**Divagation:** A digression. From a Latin word meaning *wandering about*.

**Doctrine of Recollection:** This is one of Plato's philosophical theories. In a previous existence, in the spirit world, the soul knew everything. At birth, the soul loses this knowledge, but recovers it, during this life, through great effort. Wordsworth, in his "Ode on Intimations of Immortality," discusses this theory poetically:

Our birth is but a sleep and a forgetting.

**Dogmatic:** Assertive: presumably authoritative. From a Greek word meaning *to think*.

**Doxographers:** Scholars who wrote histories of philosophy and compiled philosophical anthologies. From two Greek words meaning *writing about opinions*.

**Doxology:** A group of religious hymns glorifying God. From two Greek words meaning *the study of praise*.

# E

**Ebullient:** Effervescing: excited. From a Latin word meaning *to bubble up*.

**Eccentric:** Odd: queer. From two Greek words meaning *from the centre*.

**Ecclesiastic:** Relating to the Church. From a Greek word meaning *a popular assembly* of Athenians, where the citizens exercised their political privileges.

**Eclectic:** Selective. This expression is regularly used in philosophical writing to describe a person who does not adhere to one philosophical system, but selects dominant features from a number of systems. The term derives from a Greek word meaning *to choose*. The Roman philosopher Cicero was an eclectic.

**Effigy:** An image: a likeness. From a Latin word meaning *an image*.

**Egoism (also Egotism):** An excessive belief and interest in oneself. From the Latin word ego, meaning *I*.

**Eleemosynary:** Charitable. From a Latin word meaning *alms*.

**Elegiac:** Relating to elegy: to death. From a Greek word meaning *a lament for the dead*. The classical poets wrote commemorative or consolatory verses, in connection with the dead, in a special medium called elegiac verse.

**Eleusinian:** The Eleusinian Mysteries, celebrated every four years by the Athenians, were mystic religious ceremonies held at Eleusis in Attica.

**Elusive:** Evasive: fugitive. From a Latin word meaning *playing away*.

**Elysium:** Elysium. The famous avenue in Paris, Les Champs Elysées, has the same significance. In Greek mythology, Elysium was the final restingplace of the blessed.

**Emanate:** To originate: to stem from. From two Latin words meaning *to flow out*.

**Empirical:** Based on experiment, experience. From a Greek word meaning *experiment*.

**Encomium:** A eulogy: praise: a panegyric. From two Greek words meaning *in a revel*.

**Encyclopedia:** A book embracing a large number of fields of learning. From three Greek words meaning *learning in a circle*.

**Encyclopedist:** The first Roman encyclopedist, whose works ranged over many fields of knowledge, was M. Terentius Varro, who flourished in the first century B.C. He produced over 600 books, covering some 74 different subjects.

**End of the State is the Good Life:** This dictum is Aristotle's view of the political ideal.

**Endure and Abjure:** This is the fundamental precept of the Stoic philosopher Epictetus, who flourished in the second century A.D.

**Enigma:** A puzzling saying: an obscurity of any kind. From a Greek word meaning *speaking darkly*.

**Enthusiasm:** Ecstasy: eagerness. From two Greek words meaning *inspired by the god*.

**Enthymeme:** A syllogism consisting of only two propositions. From a Greek word meaning *keeping in mind*.

**Epexegetic (epexegetical):** Explanatory: interpretative. From a Greek word meaning *to interpret*.

**Ephebic:** An ephebic oath is taken by college graduands. From a Greek word meaning *a youth entering manhood*.

**Ephemeral:** Lasting only one day: transitory: trifling. From a Greek word meaning *a day*. Aristotle mentions certain insects whose span of life is one day.

**Ephor:** In Sparta, magistrates who, in addition to other functions, exercised judicial and executive powers. From a Greek word meaning *an overseer, a guardian.*

**Epic:** An epic is a long narrative poem, written in elevated style, on a majestic theme, packed with incident, and dominated by one particular hero or protagonist. The word epic stems from a Greek term meaning *word, speech.* Among famous national epics are:

Greek: Iliad and Odyssey.
Latin: Aeneid: Pharsalia.
Finnish: Kalewala.
French: La Chanson de Roland.
Spanish: El Cid.
English: Milton's "Paradise Lost."
Italian: Dante's "Divine Comedy."
Byzantine: Digenes Acritas.
Hindu: Mahabharata.
Persian: Shahnama of Firdausi: Mathnawi of Jalal al-din-i-Rumi.

**Epicedium:** In Latin literature, a poem eulogizing a deceased person: a dirge. From a Greek word meaning *funereal.*

**Epicene:** Relating to either sex: of common gender. From a Greek word meaning *common.*

**Epichorial:** Associated with the country, local. From two Greek words meaning *over the country.*

**Epideictic:** Intended for display or exhibition. From a Greek word meaning *to display.*

**Epigram:** A witty, pithy saying. From two Greek words meaning *writing on.*

**Epilogue:** The end of a speech: in a drama, the concluding speech: a conclusion. From two Greek words meaning *saying in addition.*

**Epimenides:** A Cretan who was a kind of Rip Van Winkle among the Greeks.

**Epiphany:** The visible manifestation of a divinity, as in the

Homeric and the Latin epics. From a Greek word meaning *appearance*.

**Episode:** An incident. In Greek tragic drama, it meant dialogue between the actors, interposed between the choral chants.

**Epistemology:** The study or theory of knowledge. From two Greek words meaning *the study of knowledge*.

**Epitaph:** An inscription on a tomb. From two Greek words meaning *on a tomb*.

**Epithalamium:** A song or poem in honor of a wedding. From two Greek words meaning *on a bridal chamber*. A famous Latin epithalamium was the *Epithalamium* of the Roman poet Claudian, in honor of the marriage of Honorius and Maria.

**Epithet:** An adjective: a descriptive word. From two Greek words meaning *to put on*.

**Epitome:** A summary: an abridgement. From two Greek words meaning *cutting into*.

**Epoch:** A period of time: an era. From a Greek word meaning *to check*.

**Epyllion:** A short epic: a short poem that has the characteristics of an epic. Vergil's "Culex," for instance, is in the nature of an epyllion. From a Greek word meaning *a small epic*.

**Equivocate:** To talk ambiguously: to prevaricate. From two Latin words meaning *to call equally*.

**Erotic:** Relating to love. Eros was the Greek god of love, son of Aphrodite. Among the Romans he was identified with Cupid.

**Eschatology:** The doctrine relating to death and immortality. From two Greek words meaning *the study of the last things*.

**Esoteric:** Obscure, abstruse, private, secret. This expression, usually applied to mystic or metaphysical matters, stems from a Greek word meaning *inner*.

**Ethics:** The science or study of morals. From a Greek word meaning *custom*.

**Ethnic:** Racial. From a Greek word meaning *a nation.*

**Etymology:** The origin of words: the derivation of words: the study of derivations. From two Greek words meaning *the study of words.*

**Eugenics:** The science of improving the breed of human beings. From a Greek word meaning *well born.*

**Euhemerus:** A Greek of the third century B.C. who developed a philosophical theory that the gods worshipped among men were originally great heroes or kings. The euhemeristic interpretation of mythology assumes this view adumbrated by Euhemerus.

**Eulogize:** To praise: to extol. From two Greek words meaning *speaking well.*

**Eunomia:** In Greek, the meaning is *a state of being well-governed.* This term is applied to Sparta, that trained its citizens for the common good.

**Eupeptic:** Relating to easy digestion: having good digestion. From two Greek words meaning *good digestion.*

**Euphemism:** The expression of something offensive or unpleasant by means of innocuous words. From two Greek words meaning *to speak well.*

**Euphoria:** A feeling of well-being. From two Greek words meaning *bearing well.*

**Euthanasia:** A 'mercy killing' in the case of chronic sufferers. The word stems from two Greek words meaning *an easy death.*

**Evangelist:** A messenger of the Gospel: a peripatetic missionary. From a Greek word meaning *a bringer of good news.*

**Excoriate:** To flay, figuratively: to scourge. From two Latin words meaning *to* (take) *off the hide.*

**Exculpate:** To pardon, to vindicate, to free from blame. From two Latin words meaning *from blame.*

**Excursus:** A digression containing explanatory matter: an appendix. From a Latin word meaning *running out.*

**Exegesis:** Interpretation: explanation: usually used in relation to Biblical commentary. From a Greek word meaning *to interpret*.

**Exegete:** A commentator: an expounder: usually used in relation to sacred literature. From a Greek word meaning *to interpret*.

**Exigency:** Urgency: necessity: demands. From a Latin word meaning *to demand*.

**Exigent:** Demanding: urgent. From a Latin word meaning *to demand*.

**Exodus:** A departure. In Greek drama, the exodus was the stage action after the final choral ode called the stasimon.

**Exorbitant:** Excessive. From two Latin words meaning *out of bounds*.

**Expediency:** The condition of achieving a purpose without moral scruples: self-interest. From a Latin word meaning *to release, to free*.

**Expedient:** A stratagem: a device. From a Latin word meaning *to free, to release*. In an adjectival sense, expedient means advisable, advantageous.

**Expedite:** To hasten: to accelerate. From a Latin word meaning *to extricate*.

**Extirpate:** To uproot: to destroy. From two Latin words meaning *from the root*.

**Extraneous:** Irrelevant: foreign. From a Latin word meaning *outside, beyond*.

# F

**Fabian:** A Fabian policy is a policy that advocates reform by slow, non-violent changes. The expression derives from Quintus Fabius Maximus, a Roman general whose delaying tactics in conflict with the Carthaginian general Hannibal earned him the nickname of Cunctator—the Delayer.

**Factitious:** Unreal: artificial. From a Latin word meaning *to make.*

**Factotum:** A person who performs all kinds of odd jobs: a handy man. From two Latin words meaning *doing everything.* In Petronius' "Cena Trimalchionis" Trimalchio calls his wife Fortunata topanta, the Greek equivalent of factotum.

**Fallacy:** A wrong idea: a logical weakness: a mistake. From a Latin word meaning *deceitful.*

**Fanaticism:** An excessive enthusiasm, originally used in a religious sense, but now of wider denotation. From a Latin word meaning *a shrine.*

**Farrago:** A jumble, a confusion. The Latin word farrago, which etymologically meant a mixture of cattle food, acquired the meaning of a jumble, or a confusion.

**Fatal:** Associated with fate: disastrous. The term stems from the Latin Fata, *the Fates.*

**Fatalist:** A person who, believing that the course of his life is pre-ordained by fate, is resigned to every situation. Kismet, the Islamic concept of fate, implies the same viewpoint.

**Fate:** Destiny: stems from the Latin fatum, or, in the plural, fata, meaning *fate.* In ancient mythology, Fate was personified as three sisters, who controlled human and divine life. One sister, Clotho, held the distaff. Lachesis spun the thread of life, while Atropos cut the thread. Compare Milton's poem "Lycidas":

> Comes the blind fury with the abhorréd shears
> And slits the thin-spun life.

**Fated:** Ordained, destined. The word stems from the Latin Fata, *the Fates.*

**Father of Ethics:** This title is applied to the Greek philosopher Socrates.

**Father of Geography:** This title is applied to Hecataeus of

Miletus, a fifth century B.C. Greek who wrote a Description of the Earth.

**Father of History:** The Greek historian Herodotus, who in the fifth century B.C. wrote an account of the Persian Wars, dealing with the conflict between the Greeks and the Persians, was so called by Cicero. His narrative, packed with strange and fascinating tales, is still extant.

**Father of Naturalism:** This title is applied to the Greek philosopher Aristotle.

**Father of Pastoral Poetry:** This designation is usually applied to Theocritus, a Greek poet who wrote on rustic life.

**Father of Philosophy:** This title is applied to the Greek philosopher Thales, who flourished in the sixth century B.C.

**Fatuous:** Stupid. From a Latin word meaning *stupid*.

**Fauna:** The animals indigenous to a country. In classical mythology, a faun was a rustic god, half man, half goat, similar to a satyr, who acted as an attendant to Pan.

**Female Homer:** This description was applied to the Greek poetess Anyte of Tegea, who flourished in the third century B.C.

**Feral:** Wild: savage: animal-like. From a Latin word meaning *a wild animal*.

**Forensic:** Relating to public discussion, particularly to legal matters. Forensic medicine, for instance, deals with medical matters in their legal aspects. Among the Romans, the forum was a public place where judicial and social business was conducted.

**Fortuitous:** Casual, accidental. From a Latin word meaning *chance*.

**Founder of Perspective:** Anaxagoras, who flourished in the fifth century B.C. wrote on perspective in theatrical scene painting.

**Frustration:** Obstruction: prevention. From a Latin word meaning *vainly*.

**Furies:** In Greek mythology, avenging goddesses. Euphemistically, and for apotropaic purposes, the Furies are often called Eumenides, the Kindly Ones.

**Furtive:** Stealthy: secret. From a Latin word meaning *stealthily*.

# G

**Gadfly of Athens:** A self-description of Socrates, who declared that his function was to goad the Athenians along analytical lines of thought in search of truth.

**Ganymedes:** A Trojan youth who was borne aloft by an eagle to be cupbearer to Jupiter. The name, which became equated with pathicus, among the Greeks and, later, the Romans, was finally corrupted into the Latin catamitus, from which stems the English catamite.

**Gastronomy:** The art of eating well, of being a gourmet. From two Greek words meaning *rules about the stomach.*

**Gastrophetes:** An ancient Greek cross-bow, invented by Zopyrus. From two Greek words meaning *bearing in the stomach.*

**Genuflection:** A bending of the knee, particularly in a religious sense. From two Greek words meaning *bending the knee.*

**Germane:** Relevant: pertinent. From a Latin word meaning *a brother, kin.*

**Gerontocracy:** Rule by old men. From two Greek words meaning *old men ruling.*

**Gerontology:** The study of old age. From two Greek words meaning *the study of old age.*

**Gerousia:** A Greek word meaning the legislative body in Sparta.

**Gnomic:** Relating to proverbial expressions; to aphorisms. From a Greek word meaning *a maxim.* In Greek literature, the gnomic poets were poets whose writings were aphoristic.

**God:** Aristotle's definition of God, as the supreme first cause, is: first moving principle, itself unmoved. In philosophical theory, this definition is known under its Latin designation as the primum mobile immobile.

**God is always doing geometry:** This expression is a Platonic concept, implying the mathematical importance in the scheme of the cosmos.

**Golden Bough:** A periapt or talisman. In Vergil's "Aeneid," the hero Aeneas presents the golden bough to Proserpina, queen of the Underworld, in order to gain entrance.

**Gordian Knot:** 'To cut the Gordian knot' means to solve a difficulty abruptly, daringly. A certain King Gordius of Phrygia in Asia tied a complicated knot in a cord attached to an ox-cart. An oracle declared that anyone undoing the knot would rule Asia. Alexander the Great cut the knot with his sword, thus fulfilling the prophecy.

**Grace, graceful:** These expressions derive from the three goddesses, the Graces Thalia, Aglaia, and Euphrosyne, who bestowed charm and beauty on human beings.

**Graces, trying to find an imperishable temple, have chosen the soul of Aristophanes:** This encomium of the lofty courage of the Greek comedy writer is traditionally attributed to Plato.

**Grand Old Man:** The original Latin expression—praegrandis senex—was applied by the Roman satirist Persius, who flourished in the first century A.D., to the Greek comedy writer Aristophanes.

**Gymnasium:** A place of athletic exercise. In ancient Greece, it was a place where athletes, dancers, and poets held public performances. The expression stems from a Greek word meaning *to exercise naked.*

**Gymnopaedia:** A Greek festival at which naked youths danced and fought in contests. From two Greek words meaning *naked youths.*

**Gymnosophist:** An adherent of a certain ascetic philosophic system. From two Greek words meaning *naked philosopher*. In his march across Asia, Alexander the Great found such philosophers in India.

# H

**Hades:** The Lower World, the abode of the spirits of the dead. In Homer, Hades is the god of the Lower Regions. Later, the term became synonymous with the location itself.

**Haematologist:** An expert in blood conditions. From two Greek words meaning *the study of blood*.

**Hagiography:** Biographies of Saints. From two Greek words meaning *holy writing*.

**Halcyon Days:** This expression was applied to a period of seven days before and seven days after the shortest day in the year, when the sea was continuously calm. According to ancient mythology, it was the period during which the halcyons, or kingfishers, nested.

**Hamartia:** A Greek word meaning a *fault* or *flaw*. This expression, used in Aristotelian literary criticism, refers to the characterial defect in a prominent character, in Greek tragic drama, that causes his downfall.

**Happiness:** In Aristotelian philosophical theory, happiness is a harmony produced by the full exercise of man's powers.

**Harpy:** A repulsively greedy person. Harpies were monsters of half-bird, half-woman form.

**Heart:** According to Aulus Gellius, a Roman anecdotist and grammarian of the second century A.D., the ancient Roman poet Ennius said he had three hearts, because he could speak Greek, Oscan, and Latin.

**Heavenly Council:** In ancient mythology, this council consisted of six female and six male deities. The female deities were Ceres, Diana, Juno, Minerva, Venus, Vesta. The male deities were: Apollo, Jupiter, Mars, Mercury, Neptune, Vulcan.

**Hecatomb:** A Greek word meaning *a sacrifice of one hundred bulls.*

**Hector:** 'To hector' means to bully. Hector was one of the Trojan leaders in the Trojan War. Homer describes him as of noble character. Hence the modern expression has acquired—as happens frequently—an unfavorable or pejorative sense.

**Hedonism:** A philosophical system that teaches pleasure as the supreme good. The expression derives from a Greek word meaning *pleasure.* The philosopher Epicurus advocated this doctrine, but his interpretation of pleasure was not sensual.

**Hegemony:** Leadership, domination. From a Greek word meaning *leadership.*

**Hellenic:** Relating to Greece: of Greek origin or influence. In Greek, Hellas means *Greece.*

**Helots:** In Sparta, the serfs, whose large numbers and frequent attempts to revolt created civic disturbances, were called helots. From a Greek word meaning *a bondsman, a captive.*

**Herculean:** Heroic, superhuman. In ancient mythology, Hercules performed twelve supremely difficult tasks.

**Heretic:** A person who maintains a religious doctrine contrary to accepted doctrine. In general, any non-conformist. From a Greek word meaning *choosing.*

**Hermaphrodite:** In ancient mythology, a bisexual divinity. From two names: Hermes and Aphrodite. Short poems on this subject appear in Ausonius and later mediaeval poets, among them Luxorius.

**Hermeneutics:** The study of interpretation. In a theological sense, the field of exegesis. From a Greek word meaning *to interpret.*

**Hermetica:** A body of ancient Greek and Latin writings of a philosophical and religious nature, attributed to Hermes Trismegistus—Hermes the Thrice Greatest, and belonging in the third century A.D.

**Hermetically:** 'Hermetically sealed' means made air-tight. The expression stems from Hermes Trismegistus—the Greek name for the Egyptian god Thoth, whose teachings were absorbed by the mediaeval alchemists.

**Hermit:** A recluse: a person who, generally from religious impulses, lives in solitude. From a Greek word meaning *solitary*.

**Hetaera (Hetaira):** A Greek word meaning *a woman companion, a paramour.*

**Heterodox:** Non-conforming: heretical. From two Greek words meaning *other opinion.*

**Heterogeneous:** Different: dissimilar. From two Greek words meaning *other kind.*

**Hexameter:** A line of verse consisting of six feet. From two Greek words meaning *six measures.*

**Hiatus:** A gap: an opening. In ancient metrics, a gap produced when a word ending in a vowel is followed by a word beginning with a vowel. From a Latin word meaning *a gap.*

**Hieratic:** Consecrated, priestly. From a Greek word meaning *sacred.*

**Hieroglyphics:** Picture characters, such as those in use among the ancient Egyptians. From two Greek words meaning *sacred carving.*

**Hierophant:** A priest. From two Greek words meaning *showing sacred things.* In the mysteries of Eleusis, the hierophantes was the chief priest.

**Hippocratic Oath:** The oath taken by medical students on graduation, in memory of Hippocrates, the Greek Father of Medicine.

**Hippodamus:** A Greek architect of the fifth century who was the first town planner. He designed the Piraeus, the Athenian harbor.

**Hippodrome:** An arena used for equestrian and other sporting performances. The term derives from two Greek words meaning *a race course.*

**Hippophile:** loving horses: one who loves horses. From two Greek words meaning *loving horses.*

**Historiography:** The writing of history. From two Greek words meaning *writing history.*

**History:** An account of events, institutions, persons, fields of knowledge: a narrative. The term derives from a Greek word meaning *investigation, inquiry.*

**Histrionic:** Dramatic: theatrical. From a Latin word meaning *an actor.*

**Holocaust:** A catastrophe involving great loss of human life. The word stems from two Greek words meaning *burning the whole* and signifying a sacrifice in which cattle were completely consumed.

**Holograph:** A document written in the handwriting of the person assumed to be the author. From two Greek words meaning *entirely written.*

**Homeric:** Mighty, vast, of epic grandeur. The word derives from the Greek poet Homer, whose epics, the Iliad and the Odyssey, are packed with zestful adventures and lusty episodes.

**Homeric Question:** Was there actually a poet called Homer? When did he live? Did he write both the Iliad and the Odyssey? These problems constitute the Homeric Question. In antiquity, as early as the third century B.C., there were critics who held the view that the Iliad and the Odyssey were written by different poets. These scholars were called chorizontes—Separators. This tradition lasted for centuries, although there were opponents. In 1795 a German scholar, F. A. Wolf, reasserted the views of the ancient Separators.

In 1921, however, Professor John Scott, in "The Unity of Homer," declared that there is one authorship for both epics. Those who hold this view, which is the general contemporary view, are called Unitarians.

**Homer of Tragedy:** This designation was applied to the Greek dramatist Sophocles, whose characters are varied, complex, and depicted with Homeric understanding and subtlety.

**Homily:** A sermon: a discourse on a moral question. From two Greek words meaning *the same crowd*.

**Homogeneous:** Of the same kind. From two Greek words meaning *the same kind*.

**Hoplite:** In ancient Greece, a fully-armed infantryman. From a Greek word meaning *a weapon*.

**Hoplomachia:** In Rome, a gladiatorial combat. From two Greek words meaning *a battle of soldiers*.

**Hospitality:** Friendly treatment: guestship, as Charles Doughty calls it. From a Latin word meaning *a guest* or *host*.

**Humanity:** The characteristics of a cultivated person. The humanities are those studies that are basically cultural. The Latin word humanus means *relating to man*. In Edinburgh University, Scotland, the Professor of Latin holds the Chair of Humanity.

**Hybris:** Excessive arrogance or pride, punished by Nemesis. Hybris is the Latinized form of the Greek word for *pride*. This weakness or sin is prominent throughout ancient Greek literature, particularly in the tragic drama.

**Hylozoism:** A philosophical concept that postulates matter as alive, that life or the cause of things is inherent in matter. From two Greek words meaning *material* and *life*. Among the Old Ionian philosophers who formulated this view were Thales and Anaximander.

**Hymeneal:** Relating to marriage. Hymen was the Greek god of marriage.

**Hymn:** A sacred song. From a Greek word meaning *a sung invocation to a god*.

**Hypnotic:** Sleep-inducing. In Greek mythology, Hypnus was the god of sleep.

**Hypocrite:** A dissembler, a false pretender. The expression stems from two Greek words meaning *pretend*. The first actor in Greek drama was called hypocrites.

**Hypothesis:** A supposition: an assumption. From two Greek words meaning *a supposition*.

**Hysteron proteron:** An inversion of order: putting the cart before the horse. In Greek the two words mean *the last first*.

# I

**I ad Graecum Pi:** This Latin phrase means *Go to the devil— Go and hang yourself:* literally, Go to the Greek Pi—because the Greek letter Pi resembles a gallows.

**Iambic:** Relating to iambic metre. The iamb is a foot consisting of a short syllable followed by a long syllable.

**Iambic Poets:** Such poets used scurrilous invective in their poems, that were written in iambic metre. They were first called iambic poets by the Greek poet Archilochus, of the seventh century B.C., himself an iambic poet.

**Iambic verse:** In poetry, a line consisting of feet containing a short syllable followed by a long one: indicated thus: ŭ ū.

**Ichor:** The Greek word ichor means the *fluid* or *blood* of the gods.

**Ichthyophagi:** A primitive people who, according to the ancient geographers, lived on sea food. The term derives from two Greek words meaning *fish eating*. Similarly, anthropophagi means *man eating*, or *cannibals*.

**Ideological:** Relating to ideas, to theories. From two Greek words meaning *studying concepts*.

**Ides:** The thirteenth, or, in some months, the fifteenth day of the month, according to the Roman calendar. The most famous Ides was the Ides of March—March 15—when Julius Caesar was assassinated.

**Idiosyncrasy:** Peculiarity. From two Greek words meaning *peculiar mingling together.*

**Idrotobolic:** This epithet, which comes from two Greek words meaning *throwing off perspiration,* was given in 1848 to a newly invented high hat, which was all the rage in London.

**Idyl:** A poetic or prose sketch of pastoral life. From a Greek word meaning *a little form.*

**Illusive:** Deceptive. From a Latin word meaning *to deceive.*

**Imminent:** Threatening: impending: approaching. From a Latin word meaning *to threaten.*

**Immunity:** Exemption: freedom from prescribed tasks or obligations. From two Latin words meaning *not obliging.*

**Impecunious:** needy: poor. From two Latin words meaning *not* (having) *money.*

**Imperturbable:** Self-controlled: calm. From Latin words meaning *not able to be affected.*

**Implacable:** Unable to be appeased: ruthless. From Latin words meaning *unable to be appeased.*

**Imprecation:** A curse. From a Latin word meaning *a prayer.*

**Impugn:** To question the truth: to assail. From two Latin words meaning *to fight against.*

**Incubation:** In ancient medical practice, incubation meant sleeping in or near a temple for curative purposes. From a Latin word meaning *to lie down.*

**Indigent:** Poor: destitute. From a Latin word meaning *needy.*

**Ineluctable:** Inevitable: unable to be overcome. In ancient drama, often applied to fate. From two Latin words meaning *not to be struggled against.*

**Iniquitous:** Wicked. From two Latin words meaning *not just.*

**In medias res:** A Latin expression meaning *into the middle of things.* This is a dramatic technique, first used in Homer, in which the author plunges into the middle of a story and then, by means of flashbacks, reconstitutes the entire chronological sequence.

**Interregnum:** A period between the vacancy of a throne and the succession: an interval of any kind. From two Latin words meaning *between the dominion*.

**Intransigence:** Irreconcilability. From Latin words meaning *not able to come to terms*.

**Invalidate:** To weaken: to nullify. From a Latin word meaning *weak*.

**Invidious:** Arousing envy: discriminatory. From a Latin word meaning *to envy*.

**Ionians:** The Greeks who had settled in Ionia, in Asia Minor, became so notable both intellectually and commercially that the non-Greeks called all Greeks Ionians.

**Ipse dixit:** A categorical assertion. The Latin words mean *he himself said so*. The expression is applied to Pythagoras and implies authoritative finality.

**Isagogic:** Relating to introductory informative compositions in various fields of learning. From a Greek word meaning *introduction*.

**Ithacan:** Ulysses was called the Ithacan because his home was in Ithaca. Similarly, Apollo was the Delian bard, having been born on Delos: Mercury, the Cyllenian, having been born on Mt. Cyllene: Venus, the Cytherean, having risen from the sea foam near the island of Cythera.

**Itinerant:** Traveling: journeying. An itinerant preacher travels about the country. From a Latin word meaning *a journey*.

**Itinerary:** A journey: a plan for a journey: a record of a journey. From a Latin word meaning *a journey*.

**It is an art to conceal art:** This is a translation of a poetic maxim—enunciated by the Roman poet Horace—that advocates literary restraint.

# J

**Jocund:** Merry: cheerful: bright. From a Latin word meaning *pleasant*. In "L'Allegro," Milton has:

> the jocund rebecks sound.

**Jovial:** Cheerful. Astrologically, the word is associated with the temperamental influence of the planet Jupiter—who is also Jove, the chief of the gods.

**Judgment of Paris:** The award of the golden apple, by the Trojan Paris to Aphrodite, the goddess of beauty.

**June:** This month, popular as a wedding month, is associated with Juno, the Roman goddess who presided over women's interests.

**Junoesque:** Majestic, statuesque. The reference is to the Roman goddess Juno, wife and sister of Jupiter. In Greek, she is Hera. Juno presided over marriage, and her name is associated with June: hence the popularity of June brides.

**Jurisprudence:** The science or study of law. From two Latin words meaning *foresight in law*.

# K

**Kalends:** The Roman word Kalendae signified the first day of each month. 'On the Greek Kalends' means *never,* since the Greek did not have Kalends.

**Kinetic:** Relating to motion: active. From a Greek word meaning *to move*.

**Know Thyself:** This advice in self-examination has been variously attributed: to the Oracle at Delphi, and to the Greek philosophers, among them Thales. The injunction was said to have been inscribed on the Temple of Apollo at Delphi.

**Kudos:** A Greek word, used without change in English, meaning *glory*. In the Homeric poems kudos, personal military prowess, was the primary motivating force.

# L

**Labyrinth:** A maze, a confusion. Labyrinth derives from the Cretan structure, of complicated design, called labyrinth, that housed a monster known as the Minotaur.

**Lachrymose:** Tearful. From a Latin word meaning *tears*.

**Laconic:** Terse, concise. The word derives from the Greek Laconia, another name for Sparta. The Spartans were noted for their concise simplicity of speech.

**Lapidary:** Relating to stones, to inscriptions on stone: a dealer or worker in precious stones. From a Latin word meaning *a stone*.

**Lares et Penates:** The lares and penates were minor Roman divinities who presided over hearth and home. In English, the Latin phrase Lares et Penates implies domestic interests.

**Lascivious:** Lustful: lewd. From a Latin word meaning *wanton*.

**Laughing Philosopher:** A designation applied in ancient tradition to the Greek philosopher Democritus, who viewed metaphysical theories with a certain humorous indulgence.

**Laurel:** A laurel wreath was granted to successful candidates in the ancient literary and athletic contests. 'To win laurels' means to acquire a reputation in some particular field.

**Laws are the conventions of an older generation:** This dictum was enunciated by Hippias, a fifth century Greek Sophist.

**Laws of Lycurgus:** Lycurgus was a Spartan king who enacted scrupulously just laws. His name, like that of Solon, is associated with wise, balanced legislation.

**Legend:** An unauthenticated story: an inscription, heading, or explanation. From a Latin word meaning *something that is to be read.*

**Legislate:** To enact laws. From two Latin words meaning *to pass laws.*

**Leisure without study is death:** A saying of Seneca, the Roman Stoic philosopher who flourished in the reign of Nero.

**Lesbian:** The Greek poetess Sappho, who flourished in the ninth century B.C., belonged to the island of Lesbos. Since she was known for her close friendship with females, the term Lesbian now has a perverted sexual connotation.

**Lesion:** An injury. From a Latin word meaning *to injure.*

**Lethean:** Producing forgetfulness. In Greek mythology, Lethe was a river in Hades from which the spirits of the dead drank, to ensure oblivion of their past.

**Lexicographer:** A person who compiles a dictionary. From two Greek words meaning *writing a dictionary.*

**Lexicon:** A dictionary. From a Greek term meaning *a word book.*

**Libation:** A pouring out, usually of wine, in honor of a divinity. From a Latin word meaning *to pour out.*

**Library:** A place devoted to books. The expression stems from two Latin words meaning *a storeroom for books.* The first public library is said to have been founded by the Greek tyrant Pisistratus in Athens, in the sixth century B.C.

**Ligneous:** Of wood, woody. From a Latin word meaning *wood.*

**Liturgical:** Relating to prayer or public worship. From a Greek word meaning *public worship.*

**Live hidden:** This was the favorite saying of Epicurus. It means: Live a life withdrawn from public activities.

**Logic:** The study of valid reasoning: valid reasoning. From a Greek word meaning *relating to speech* or *reason.*

**Lotos Eater:** A person who lives in easeful idleness. The origi-

nal lotos eaters were Odysseus' sailors who came to a land
—sometimes identified with the island of Djerba, off the
coast of North Africa—where, on eating the lotos—identified with the Arabic Nebk, a kind of crab-apple, from which
a juice is distilled—they forgot their past, their longing to
return home. Alfred Tennyson's poem, "The Lotos-Eaters,"
deals with the same theme.

**Love by Fission:** In one of the Platonic Dialogues Plato pokes
fun at the comedy writer Aristophanes, who declares that
human beings were originally of spherical shape, endowed
with four arms and legs, and effected love by fission.

**Lucifer:** The Latin name for the planet Venus. The term
means *light bringer*. In Greek Lucifer is identified with
Phosphorus, which also means light bringer. In later, Christian literary and religious tradition, Lucifer is synonymous
with Satan.

**Lucretius:**                                    he denied
                    Divinely the divine, and died
                    Chief poet on the Tiber-side.

These lines, from Elizabeth B. Browning's "A Vision of
Poets," refer to the Roman poet Lucretius, whose theme was
the material nature of the universe.

**Lucubration:** Night labor: night study: work produced by
laborious night study. From a Latin word meaning *light*
(of a lamp).

**Lucullan:** Lavish, luxurious. A Lucullan banquet is one fit
for Lucullus. Lucullus was a Roman general, of the first
century B.C., who was a gourmet and spent large sums in
gastronomic entertainment.

**Lustration:** In the religious rites in Rome, a purification occurring every five years. From a Latin word meaning *washing*.

**Lyceum:** A place of learning or of entertainment. The Lyceum was the school founded in Athens by Aristotle for the study of philosophy.

**Lyric:** A lyric is a poem expressing the poet's personal feelings. The word is associated with a Greek term meaning *lyre*, because such poems were sung to the accompaniment of a lyre.

# M

**Macerate:** To pound: to soften: to wear away. From a Greek word meaning *to knead.*

**Maecenas:** A maecenas is a wealthy patron of the arts. Maecenas, a Roman who flourished in the first century B.C., was a liberal patron of the distinguished literary figures of his time—among them Vergil and Horace.

**Maenads:** In ancient mythology, women who, under Dionysiac influence, were driven into frenzy.

**Mandate:** An order: an injunction. From a Latin word meaning *to entrust.* In Imperial Rome, mandata were formal instructions given to a Roman provincial governor by the Emperor.

**Manes:** A Latin word meaning *spirits of the dead.* Roman funereal inscriptions often bore the letters D M S: sacred to the god spirits of the dead.

**Man is the measure of all things:** This dictum was enunciated by Protagoras, a fifth century Greek Sophist.

**Manumission:** Emancipation: liberation. From two Latin words meaning *to send forth from one's hand.* Manumission was the Roman procedure by means of which slaves acquired their freedom.

**Marathon:** A race. Marathon was a plain in Attica where the Persians were defeated by the Greeks in 490 B.C. Pheidippides ran all the way to Athens, a distance of some twenty four miles, to report the victory. This incident is rousingly described in Robert Browning's poem "Pheidippides."

**Martial:** Warlike, fond of war. The expression is associated with Mars, the Roman god of war.

**Martyr:** A person who suffers agony or death rather than renounce his religion: one who makes sacrifices for an ideal. From a Greek word meaning *a witness*.

**Master of those who know:** Dante thus calls the Greek philosopher Aristotle.

**Materfamilias:** This Latin word, used in English without any change, means *the mistress* or *mother of a household*.

**Mathematics:** This term, now applied exclusively to the science of numbers and calculation, stems from a Greek word meaning *subjects of instruction*. Pythagoras, it is said, first applied the word in its restricted numerological sense.

**Matter is indestructible:** A principle enunciated by the fifth century Greek philosopher Anaxagoras.

**Mausoleum:** A tomb. Mausolus was an ancient king of Asia Minor whose queen, Artemisia, had a large, elaborately decorated building erected in his memory. The structure was set up at Halicarnassus, in the fourth century B.C.

**Mean:** In Aristotelian philosophy, a concept that teaches moderation, a middle course, in human conduct. The Roman poet Horace calls it 'the golden mean.'

**Megapolitan:** Relating to large, overpopulated cities. From two Greek words meaning *great city*.

**Melic:** Relating to song: lyric. In a literary sense, it is used in the phrase melic poetry, a dominant genre in the history of Greek literature.

**Mendacity:** The condition of lying: a falsehood. From a Latin word meaning *false*.

**Mendicity:** The condition of begging: beggary. From a Latin word meaning *to beg*.

**Mentor:** A counselor, a guide. Mentor was the counselor of Ulysses.

**Mercenary:** A soldier who serves for pay. The term comes from a Latin word meaning *pay*. Such troops were used among the Greeks and Romans.

**Mercurial:** Volatile, temperamental. The word is associated astrologically with the planet Mercury, the ancient messenger of the gods.

**Meretricious:** Ornamental: gaudily alluring. From a Latin word meaning *a prostitute.*

**Metamorphosis:** Change of shape. From a Greek word meaning *to transform.* "The Metamorphoses" is the title of a series of poems, by the Roman poet Ovid, describing legendary transformations. The picaresque novel by the Roman Apuleius is also called "The Metamorphoses."

**Metempsychosis:** The transmigration of the soul: the passing of the soul, at death, into another body. From Greek words meaning *beyond the soul.* This doctrine was fundamental in Pythagorean philosophy.

**Metic:** An alien who resided in Attica. The expression comes from two Greek words meaning *changing residence.* The metic had no civil rights, could not hold office, vote, or claim legal protection. Nor could he own real estate or participate in Greek religious worship. On the other hand, he paid metic taxes and, according to law, was required to have a patron.

**Meticulous:** Over careful in small matters: extremely scrupulous. From a Latin word meaning *fearful, timid.*

**Metropolis:** In Greece, the parent city of a colony. From two Greek words meaning *mother city.*

**Midas Touch:** 'To have the Midas touch' means to have a faculty for acquiring wealth. In ancient mythology, Midas was a king who turned into gold whatever he touched.

**Mighty Beast:** This name was applied by Plato to the masses, influenced by Sophistic teachings.

**Mime:** Among the Romans, a mime: a farce: a scurrilous dramatic reproduction of low life. The term comes from a Greek word meaning *a mime, an imitation*. In Imperial times, female parts were acted by dissolute women, some of whom achieved literary notoriety.

**Mind:** This expression—the Greek word for mind is *nous*—was attached contemptuously to the philosopher Anaxagoras for his intellectual interests.

**Minotaur:** A monster. In classical mythology, the Minotaur, offspring of Pasiphae, the wife of King Minos, and a bull, was half man, half bull.

**Miracle:** A name applied to the poetess Sappho.

**Misogynist:** A person who hates women. From a Greek word meaning *hatred of women*. Euripides the Greek dramatist was believed to be a misogynist.

**Mitigate:** To soften: to render milder, less harsh. From a Latin word meaning *mild*.

**Mnemonic:** A memorizing device. In Greek mythology, Mnemosyne was the mother of the Muses. The Greek word mnemosyne itself means *memory*.

**Moira:** Fate. The Greek word moira means *an allotted portion*.

**Monarchy:** Rule by one person. From two Greek words meaning *rule by a single person*.

**Monograph:** A dissertation, a treatise, dealing with one topic or phase of a subject. From two Greek words meaning *one writing*.

**Monologue:** A speech or talk delivered by one person. In Greek drama, a scene in which one actor delivered a soliloquy. From two Greek words meaning *speaking alone*.

**Monopoly:** An exclusive right or privilege to control the purchase, selling, or manufacturing of a commodity. From two Greek words meaning *to sell alone*.

**Monotheism:** The doctrine that there is only one God. From two Greek words meaning *God alone*.

**Moratorium:** A national postponement of payment of a debt. The term derives from the Latin mora, *a delay*.

**Morose:** Gloomy: surly: sullen. From a Latin word meaning *character*.

**Morpheus:** 'In the arms of Morpheus' means asleep. Morpheus was the Roman god of sleep.

**Morphology:** The study of change of form. From two Greek words meaning *the study of shapes*. In biology, morphology refers to the study of the structure and form of plants and animals. In philology, it refers to changes in inflections of words.

**Most Homeric of Men:** This title was applied to the Greek historian Herodotus, for the spacious, varied, human character of his tales.

**Most tragic of historians:** This expression is applied to the Greek historian Thucydides.

**Mulct:** To punish: to fine. From a Latin word meaning *to punish*.

**Museum:** This word is associated with the Muses, the nine daughters of Jupiter who presided over art, music, learning, and dancing.

**Musical Man:** The Platonic phrase musicos aner, which means *the musical man,* embraced other studies besides music. In modern phraseology, the musicos aner would approximate a humanist.

**Myrmidon:** A minor official. Policemen are called 'myrmidons of the law.' The Myrmidones were a Thessalian tribe that participated in the Trojan War as allies of Achilles.

**Mythologos:** A teller of fables. This Greek word expresses Aristotle's estimate of Herodotus.

# N

**Natatorium:** A place for swimming: a swimming pool. From two Latin words meaning *a place for swimming.*

**Nature Does Nothing without a Purpose:** One of the principles of Aristotelian physics.

**Necromancy:** The practice of conjuring the spirits of the dead in order to hold converse with them. From two Greek words meaning *divination by exorcising the dead.*

**Nectar:** Any delicious drink. In Greek mythology, nectar was the drink of the gods.

**Nemean Games:** The games that, according to one legend, originated with Hercules after he had slain the Nemean lion. They were of a religious nature, associated with Zeus.

**Nemesis:** Retribution, punishment. Nemesis was a Greek divinity who punished excessive human pride.

**Neologism:** A word recently coined. From two Greek words meaning *a new word.*

**Nestor:** A term applied to a very old and wise person. Nestor was an aged king who appears in Homer's "Odyssey."

**Neumata:** A Latin word meaning *musical notes.* Such notes were added, by mediaeval scribes, to passages of Latin poetry, especially the Odes of Horace, so that the poem could be sung.

**Nexus:** A link: connection. The Latin word nexus means *a link.*

**Nihil ex nihilo:** A Latin expression meaning *nothing from nothing.* This is the cosmological view enunciated by the Roman poet Lucretius in his poem "The Nature of Things."

**No man can be called happy until he is dead:** According to the historian Herodotus, this dictum was uttered by the Greek philosopher Solon to King Croesus of Lydia.

**Nostalgia:** Homesickness: a longing for home. From two Greek words meaning *return home* and *pain.*

**Nothing Too Much:** This counsel, attributed to Solon, the sixth century B.C. Greek statesman, was inscribed on Apollo's temple at Delphi.

**Numismatics:** The study of coins. From a Greek word meaning *a coin.*

**Numismatist:** An expert in coins. From a Greek word meaning *a coin.*

**Nyctiphobia:** Fear of darkness. From two Greek words meaning *fear of the night.*

**Nymph:** A maiden. The Latin word nympha means a minor female divinity associated with the forests or the sea.

# O

**Obelisk:** A pillar, tapering into a pyramid. From a Greek word meaning *a pointed pillar.*

**Obese:** Stout: fat. From a Latin word meaning *fat.*

**Obfuscate:** To obscure: to confuse. From a Latin word meaning *dark.*

**Obiter dictum:** A legal opinion: an incidental remark or judgment of any kind. From two Latin words meaning *said by the way.*

**Objurgation:** Reproof: scolding. From a Latin word meaning *to scold.*

**Obliterate:** To wipe out: to efface. From two Latin words meaning *to smear off.*

**Obloquy:** Calumny: censure. From two Latin words meaning *speaking against.*

**Obscure:** A nickname applied to the fifth century B.C. Greek philosopher Heraclitus.

**Obtuse:** Dull: insensitive. From a Latin word meaning *blunted*.

**Ode:** a poem that could be set to music. From a Greek word meaning *a song*.

**Odometer:** An instrument for measuring distances. From a Greek word meaning *measuring a road*.

**Odyssey:** A pilgrimage, an adventure. The expression stems from the Greek Odysseus, the hero of Homer's epic poem "The Odyssey," who for ten years after the Trojan War experienced many strange adventures before returning home to Ithaca.

**Officious:** Meddlesome: intrusive: forward. From a Latin word meaning *duty, obligation*.

**Old Man Eloquent:** John Milton's description of the Greek orator Isocrates.

**Olfactory:** Relating to the sense of smell. From two Latin words meaning *causing to smell*.

**Oligarchy:** Derives from two Greek words meaning *government by a few*.

**Olympian:** Relating to Olympus: majestic, supreme. Mt. Olympus, in Thessaly, was the home of the ancient Greek gods.

**Olympic Games:** These games, traditionally founded in the eighth century B.C., were abolished in 394 A.D., but have been revived in modern times.. They were originally athletic, literary, and artistic contests, held every four years in honor of Zeus, at Olympia in Greece, and involved, in addition to contests, public festivities and sacrifices.

**One man, no man:** This Greek concept means that man cannot be alone. It indicates the gregariousness of the Greeks and their social impulses.

**Ontology:** The study or theory of existence or being. From two Greek words meaning *the study of being*.

**Opprobrium:** Shame: reproach. From a Latin word meaning *to reproach*.

**Optimism:** Viewing matters in the best light: a tendency to interpret occurrences in the most favorable light. From a Latin word meaning *best.*

**Oratory:** According to Cicero, the three functions of oratory are: to prove a point, to afford pleasure, and to persuade.

**Orchestra:** A section of a theatre: a group of musicians. In ancient Greece, the orchestra was a space in the theatre where the chorus danced. In Roman times, the orchestra was a section of the amphitheatre reserved for distinguished Romans. From a Greek word meaning *dance.*

**Orpheum:** A music hall or opera house: so called from Orpheus, a Thracian poet and musician whose musical powers enchanted even wild beasts.

**Orthoepy:** The study of the correct pronunciation of words. From two Greek words meaning *correct words.*

**Orthography:** The art of correct spelling. From two Greek words meaning *correct writing.*

**Oscillate:** To swing back and forth: to sway, vibrate, waver. From a Latin word meaning *to swing.*

**Ostracize:** To banish, exclude from a particular social group. In ancient Greece, the Athenians voted against a statesman by placing his name on an ostrakon, an earthenware tablet. Six thousand adverse votes constituted a decree of banishment.

**Ostrakon:** A potsherd: a fragment of pottery: a tile. From a Greek word meaning *a tablet, a tile.*

**Otiose:** Useless: unnecessary. From a Latin word meaning *leisure, ease.*

**Ovation:** A welcome: popular homage. From a Latin word meaning *to rejoice.*

**Oxymoron:** A rhetorical figure that combines contradictory words. From two Greek words meaning *sharp* and *foolish.* (See: Paradox).

# P

**Paean:** A chant of thanksgiving. First sung by the god Apollo after his defeat of the Python at Delphi.

**Paedophage:** A child-eater. From two Greek words meaning *child-eater.* In Greek mythology, Cronus was the intended paedophage of Zeus.

**Pagan:** An unbeliever: a non-Christian: a savage. From a Latin word meaning *a peasant:* hence one who is not affected by the civilizing influences of a city.

**Palaeography:** The study of ancient writings. From two Greek words meaning *ancient writings.*

**Palimpsest:** A manuscript on which the original text has been scraped off to permit another text to be imposed on the cleaned vellum. From two Greek words meaning *scraped again.*

**Palingenesis:** The doctrine of metempsychosis or the rebirth of the soul. From two Greek words meaning *born again.*

**Palinode:** A poetic retraction; a recantation, denying a statement made in a previous ode. From two Greek words meaning *a song again.*

**Palladium:** A music hall or similar place of entertainment. In Latin Palladium means an image of the goddess Pallas Athene. Such a statue stood in Troy, to preserve the safety of the city.

**Panacea:** A remedy for all ills. From two Greek words meaning *all healing.*

**Panchromatic:** Relating to all colors. From two Greek words meaning *all colors.*

**Panegyric:** A eulogy: a glorifying speech. From two Greek words meaning (a speech) *before a whole assembly.* A famous panegyric is the Panegyric on the Emperor Trajan, by Pliny the Younger. Another one is on the Emperor Majorian, by Sidonius Apollinaris.

**Panes et Circenses:** Bread and circus performances. This Latin phrase comes from the Roman satirist Juvenal, and refers to the two chief activities of the Roman populace in the first century A.D.

**Panic:** A sudden unreasoning terror. Pan was a Greek rustic god whose presence in any wild or remote spot was believed to induce a sudden, pervasive fear.

**Pankration:** A Greek athletic contest consisting of a combination of boxing and wrestling. From two Greek words meaning *all powerful.*

**Pantheism:** The doctrine that equates the universe with God. The doctrine of the philosopher Spinoza. From two Greek words meaning *everything is God.*

**Pantheon:** A Roman temple housing all the gods, built in the reign of the first Emperor, Augustus. The term comes from two Greek words meaning *all the gods.*

**Papyrus:** Papyrus, from which stems paper, was writing material made from the papyrus reed, found largely along the Nile banks.

**Parabasis:** In Greek comedy, the address of the chorus to the audience, in which the chorus expresses the poet's views.

**Paradox:** A contradiction: a self-contradictory statement. From two Greek words meaning *beyond opinion.* A famous paradox from the Roman satirist Juvenal is: Honesty is praised and starves. The paradox was a regular rhetorical technique among the ancient writers.

**Paraenetic:** Hortatory: advisory. From a Greek word meaning *to advise.*

**Paragon:** A model: an ideal type. From two Greek words meaning *to sharpen against* (a whetstone): hence to sharpen to the point of perfection.

**Parasite:** In Greece, a parasite was a poor person invited to a meal. The term comes from two Greek words meaning *beside food.* Among the Romans, a parasite was similarly a poor poet or philosopher invited to a banquet and hence inclined to flatter his host.

In modern times, the word has acquired, as often happens, a pejorative significance meaning a hanger-on, one who lives on another—the denotation extending into plant and animal life.

**Parcae:** A euphemistic and apotropaic name for the Fates. The word means *The Indulgent Ones*.

**Parnassus:** A mountain range near Delphi. In classical mythology, it was reputed to be the seat of Apollo and the Muses. Hence the expression is used figuratively to symbolize poetic or literary inspiration.

**Parodos:** In Greek drama, a passage through which the chorus enters the orchestra. It also meant the entrance of the chorus.

**Paroemiography:** The making of collections of proverbs from both prose and verse sources. From two Greek words meaning *the writing of proverbs*.

**Paronomasia:** Punning. From a Greek word meaning *to make a word by a change*.

**Parricide:** One who kills a parent: the act of killing a parent. From a Latin word meaning *killing a parent* or *near relative*.

**Parsimony:** Frugality: niggardliness. From a Latin word meaning *to spare*.

**Paterfamilias:** This Latin word, used in English without any change, means *the father of a household*.

**Pathos:** A quality that induces pity or sympathy. Pathos stems from a Greek word meaning *suffering*.

**Patrimony:** Inheritance from a father. From a Latin word meaning *father*.

**Peculation:** Stealing: misappropriation of money. From a Latin word meaning *to embezzle*.

**Pedagogue:** A teacher, a schoolmaster. From two Greek words meaning *leading a boy*. In ancient Greece the teacher was a slave who accompanied a boy to and from school.

**Pejorative:** Depreciatory. From a Latin word meaning *worse.*

**Peltasts:** Greek soldiers. From a Greek word meaning *a small shield,* their only armor.

**Pentameter:** A line of verse consisting of five feet. From two Greek words meaning *five measures.*

**Pentathlon:** An athletic contest in which each contestant participates in five events. From two Greek words meaning *five contests.*

**Peremptory:** Abrupt: brusque, decisive. From a Latin word meaning *to destroy.*

**Peripatetic:** Ambulatory. From two Greek words meaning *walking around.* The Peripatetics were the adherents of Aristotle. It is thought that Aristotle delivered his lectures while walking around the courtyard of the Lyceum.

**Peripety:** A Greek word meaning *reversal* or *change* from what was intended. This expression belongs in Aristotelian dramatic criticism, and applies to the techniques of Greek tragic drama.

**Periphery:** The circumference: the boundaries of a surface. From two Greek words meaning *carrying around.*

**Periphrasis:** A long expression that is equivalent to a short expression. Synonymous with circumlocution. From two Greek words meaning *speaking around.*

**Permanent (or stock) epithet:** A permanent or stock epithet is a descriptive expression regularly associated with a particular word. In the Homeric epics, permanent epithets occur as follows:

far-darting Apollo
rosy-fingered dawn
well-greaved Greeks
Hera the ox-eyed queen

**Peroration:** The concluding part of a speech: the summation. From two Latin words meaning *to speak to the end.*

**Perspicacious:** Keen: discerning. He was a perspicacious student. From two Latin words meaning *looking through*.

**Perspicuous:** Clear: lucid. A perspicuous assertion. From two Latin words meaning *looking through*.

**Pertinacious:** Persistent: obstinate. From a Latin word meaning *tenacious*.

**Pessimism:** Viewing matters in the worst light: a tendency to interpret occurrences in the most unfavorable light. From a Latin word meaning *worst*.

**Phaethon:** A vehicle, now obsolete. So called from Phaethon, a youth who tried to drive the chariot of the sun god.

**Phalanx:** A military formation, invented by the Greeks and later developed by the Romans into the legion. From a Greek word meaning *a battle line*.

**Phenomenon:** An occurrence: any actuality. From a Greek word meaning *to appear*.

**Philanthropy:** Love of mankind: benevolence: charitableness. From two Greek words meaning *love of men*.

**Philhellenic:** Friendly to Greece. From two Greek words meaning *loving Greece*.

**Philippics:** A philippic is a diatribe, a polemic, an oratorical invective. The term is associated with the fourth century Greek orator Demosthenes, who delivered a series of speeches against King Philip of Macedon.

**Philologist:** The first Roman philologist was L. Aelius Praeconius Stilo, who flourished in the first century B.C. He pursued investigations in Latin literature, oratory, and antiquities.

**Philosopher:** This term, without any nominal designation, has been universally applied, in the history of philosophy, to Aristotle.

**Philosophers of the Garden:** These were the adherents, both men and women, of the philosopher Epicurus, who turned his garden into his lecture headquarters.

**Plagiarism:** Passing off as one's own ideas, phrases, or more extensive literary material. From a Greek word meaning *crooked*.

**Platonic Friendship:** In his Dialogues, Plato discusses the intellectual friendship between men of disparate age and interests. On the other hand, homosexuality was a fact among the ancient Greeks. In modern days, Platonic Friendship implies heterosexual friendship free from sexual consummation.

**Platonopolis:** City of Plato. Such a city was planned in Italy, by the Emperor Gallienus in the third century A.D., as a philosopher's city.

**Plausible:** Acceptable, reasonable. From a Latin word meaning *praiseworthy*.

**Plebeian:** Relating to the people: common, vulgar. The term derives from the Latin word plebs, *the populace*.

**Plebiscite:** A decree or vote of the people. From two Latin words meaning *a decree of the people*.

**Plenipotentiary:** Having full power: a diplomat vested with full power. From two Latin words meaning *full power*.

**Pleonasm:** Redundancy: superfluity. From a Greek word meaning *to abound*. (See: Redundancy).

**Plethora:** Excess. From a Greek word meaning *being full*.

**Plutocracy:** Government by wealth. From two Greek words meaning *rule by the wealthy*.

**Plutonian:** A name given to granite, which was believed to be formed by heat in the bowels of the earth. The expression is associated with Pluto, king of the Lower Regions.

**Pneumatic:** Operated by air pressure: inflated with air. From a Greek word meaning *air, spirit, wind*.

**Poet:** The distinctive and superlative title was applied by Aristotle to Homer.

**Poet:** Dante thus describes Vergil, the Roman epic poet of the first century B.C.

**Poets:** According to Aulus Gellius, a Roman anecdotist and grammarian of the second century A.D., ancient poets were called vagabonds.

**Polemic:** A speech attacking a person: an abusive invective. From a Greek word meaning *warlike*.

**Polis:** A Greek city-state, independent in its administration, but much more than a city. It was a political centre embracing the outlying districts, whose dwellers, in their communal totality, formed the polis.

**Polyglot:** A person skilled in many tongues: a linguist. From two Greek words meaning *many tongues.*

**Polyhistor:** A scholar: a polymath: a person erudite in many fields. From a Greek word meaning *very learned.*

**Polymath:** One who has mastered many fields of knowledge. Aristotle was considered a polymath. The term comes from two Greek words meaning *knowing much.*

**Polyphony:** A musical composition involving independent but harmonizing elements: a multiplicity of sounds. From two Greek words meaning *many sounds.*

**Polytheism:** The belief in many gods. From two Greek words meaning *many gods.*

**Pontiff:** This title of the Pope stems from the Latin Pontifex, *priest.*

**Pornography:** Writing about prostitutes. From two Greek words meaning *to write* and *prostitute.* Among the Romans, the harlot was identified by an amazing variety of synonyms. In the comedies of Plautus the prostitute plays a dominant part.

Broadly speaking, there were two types of meretrix, harlot, in Rome: those who were recognized officially and had to register with the aediles and pay a tax—meretricium—for the licentia stupri, permission to function. The other class consisted of clandestine lupae—she-wolves—unregistered—who lived nowhere in particular, merely wandering through the streets, taking up positions on the steps of monuments, on public benches, at tombstones, under archways, or near aqueducts. They were known as erratica scrota.

For registered lupae there were touts—admissarii—both men and women, who accosted prospective customers in public thoroughfares and offered to guide them. In this capacity the admissarii were also known as adductores or conductores.

Professing the lupa's trade but euphemistically called by indirection were the saltatrices, dancers, the fidicinae, flute-players, and the tibicinae, lyre-players, who balanced their acknowledged musical talent with an exclusive prostitution. They were the bonae meretrices, like Cytheris, who often received at her table, among other notables, Cicero himself. They were the delictae and pretiosae, kept women for the higher social strata. These cryptic lupae were not subject to the meretricium or the licentia stupri.

Musical entertainments, banquets, social assemblies of all kinds were to Cicero synonymous with wantonness—libidines: that is, the obscene figures found on the walls of the Venereum.

There are no fewer than twenty five synonyms denoting a person of this class. Amica, mistress, appears in Plautus, Terence, and Catullus, and, later, in Tertullian. The same meaning is given domina in malam partem by two poets: Tibullus and Propertius.

In Late Latin usage we find fornicatrix, as in Isidore of Seville, Origines. Lupa was a name given to Roman prostitutes in early times, as the historian Livy mentions. The nurse of Romulus, Acca Larentia, was a lupa, a favorite prostitute of Faustulus' fellow shepherds. The dwelling of the lupa took the name of lupanar, wolf's lair, and festivals in memory of this lupa, after her death, were called Lupercalia. These festivals were suppressed by the Roman Senate on account of their license. Similarly, the Floralia were instituted in honor of the lupa Flora, according to the patristic writer Lactantius. The word lupatria is used in the sense of lupa by the novelist Petronius.

The word meretrix, used in a generic sense for a wanton of any type, is strictly a professional harlot who sells herself for merx, payment. Its use ranges all the way from Plautus to Tertullian. Moecha, of Greek origin, means an adulteress, and is so used in Catullus, Horace, and Juvenal. The poets also use pellex, a mistress, concubine, kept woman as a synonym.

Notable among the terms in that both genders are found used indifferently is prostibula, prostibulum: as in Plautus, Paulus Diaconus, and Tertullian. These prostibulae, serving the lower levels of the populace, were subdivided as follows, the variety of synonyms being evidence of the widespread, accepted nature of the condition throughout the Roman masses: alicaria, a prostitute who frequents the spelt mills: caserita, one who waits for a client at home: copa, attached to inns, which were virtually lupanaria: diabola, in Late Latin usage, a she-devil, with a religious connotation: foraria, one who frequents public thoroughfares: noctuvigila, a night hag: peregrina, one who associates with foreigners or who is herself of foreign origin: proseda, one who sits in public, similar to prostibula.

Other terms include: quadrantaria, one whose favors are very cheap—a 'quarter' of the coin as. The wife of a certain Metellus sold herself for a bath that cost a 'quarter'. vaga: one who wanders the streets: scrantia, scratta, scratia, a generic term for any prostitute: scrota, possibly for scorta by metathesis or by an inversion common in sex symbolism: scortum, a harlot: scortillum, a diminutive of scortum: these last two terms denoting a definite realization of their pejorative social effect.

Posse: A group of men vested with authority: a band of men acting under authority. From a Latin word meaning *to be able*.

**Possession for all time:** Thucydides' own view, expressed in the introduction, of the purpose of his "Peloponnesian War."

**Posthumous:** Occurring after one's death. From a Latin word meaning *last*.

**Postulate:** An axiomatic proposition: a hypothesis. The expression, which is common in speculative and scientific contexts, stems from a Latin verb meaning *to demand*.

**Precocious:** Prematurely developed. From two Latin words meaning *ripened beforehand*.

**Predicament:** A dilemma: a quandary: a perplexing situation. From a Latin word meaning *a quality, a characteristic*.

**Prelude:** Introductory matter: in music, poetry; or, analogously, introductory action. From two Latin words meaning *playing before*.

**Prevaricate:** To tell falsehoods: to lie. From a Latin word meaning *walk crookedly*.

**Priapean:** Relating to Priapus, god of fertility, symbolized by the phallus: obscene. Priapean poems are very common in Latin literature, particularly in the Silver Age and in the Middle Ages.

**Procrustean:** Stretched or adapted ruthlessly to fit a rigid need. In Greek mythology, Procrustes was an innkeeper who had one bed for guests. When the guest was too short for the bed, Procrustes stretched him. When the guest was too long, his legs were cut off to fit the bed.

**Prodigy:** An extraordinary phenomenon, or occurrence, or person. From a Latin word meaning *a portent, an omen*.

**Proemium:** An introduction: a prelude, in a literary sense. From two Greek words meaning *a song* or *poem before*.

**Proempticon:** A poem of good wishes for a safe voyage. From two Greek words meaning *sending forward*.

**Progenitor:** Ancestor: founder: forefather. From a Latin word meaning *to beget*.

**Prognostication:** Forecast: prophecy: prediction. From two Greek words meaning *to know beforehand*.

**Prolific:** Abundant: fruitful. From Latin words meaning *to make* and *offspring*.

**Prolix:** Verbose. From a Latin word meaning *extended*.

**Prologue:** A preface or introduction to a lecture, a performance, or a poem. The term stems from two Greek words meaning *an introductory speech*. In Greek drama, the prologue was the first act, preceding the entrance of the chorus.

**Promethean:** Relating to Prometheus. In classical mythology, Prometheus was a Titan who was punished by Zeus for stealing fire from heaven for mortal use. The word Prometheus itself in Greek means *forethought*.

**Propensity:** Inclination: tendency: bias. From a Latin word meaning *hanging*.

**Propitiate:** To appease: to conciliate. From a Latin word meaning *favorable*.

**Proselyte:** A convert to another religion. From a Greek word meaning *a newcomer*.

**Protagonist:** One who plays a leading part in any situation. The term derives from two Greek words meaning *first actor*.

**Protean:** Changeable, able to change form. In Greek mythology, Proteus, a sea divinity, could change his shape at will.

**Prototype:** The original: pattern. From two Greek words meaning *first model*.

Among notable classical prototypes are the following:

> **Conjugal faithfulness:** Penelope
> **Old Age:** Priam: Nestor
> **Cunning:** Ulysses
> **Companionship:** Achilles and Patroclus, Aeneas and Achates
> **Filial devotion:** Aeneas
> **A woman scorned:** Juno, Phaedra, Dido
> **Fifth columnist:** Sinon

**Martyr to principles:** Prometheus, Socrates

**Playboy:** Paris

**Conjugal Infidelity:** Clytemnestra, who was killed, along with her lover Aegisthus, by her son Orestes.

**Broken Promise:** Laomedon, king of Troy, who refused his promised reward to Apollo and Poseidon, who had built the walls of Troy.

**Prophesying in the Wilderness:** Cassandra, doomed by Apollo to prophecy without being believed.

**Seductiveness:** Calypso, who kept Ulysses for eight years.

**Filibuster:** The Roman Cato the Elder, who on every conceivable occasion advocated in the senate the destruction of Carthage.

**First Aviator:** Daedalus

**Self-made Millionaire:** Trimalchio, the freedman hero of Petronius' Banquet of Trimalchio.

**Psalm:** A sacred song. From a Greek word meaning *to play on a stringed instrument.*

**Pseudo:** False: spurious. From a Greek word meaning *lying.*

**Psychic:** Relating to the soul or spirit. The Greek word psyche means *the soul.*

**Punctilious:** Precise: exact: scrupulous. From a Latin word meaning *a point.*

**Pusillanimous:** Cowardly. From two Latin words meaning *very small mind.*

**Putative:** Presumed: supposed: deemed. From a Latin word meaning *to think.*

**Pylon:** A gateway: a tower. From a Greek word meaning *a gateway.*

**Pyrrhic:** A Pyrrhic victory is a victory gained at a disastrous cost. In the third century B.C. Pyrrhus, King of Epirus, in Greece, defeated the Romans, but his own losses were ruinous.

**Pythagorean Doctrine:** The fundamental doctrine of the philosophy of Pythagoras, whose floruit in the fifth century B.C., is that the concept of number motivates all nature.

**Pythian:** Relating to Pytho, an old name for Delphi. The Pythian Games were held every four years in honor of Apollo, destroyer of the Python.

# Q

**Quadrivium:** A Latin word meaning *a group of four*. The quadrivium embraced four of the seven arts of mediaeval education, and consisted of arithmetic, music, geometry, and astronomy.

**Quarantine:** A compulsory restraint, especially in connection with disease. From a Latin word meaning *forty*—originally the period of restraint lasted forty days.

# R

**Ratiocination:** The process of reasoning or thinking. From a Latin word meaning *to reason*.

**Realist of the Aegean:** This description, by an English translator, was applied to the third century B.C. Greek poet Herondas.

**Recidivist:** A hardened criminal. From a Latin word meaning *falling back, relapsing*.

**Recitation:** An oral recital of a literary work. In Latin, recitatio was the practice, in Imperial times, of reading part of one's literary work, prose or poetry, publicly, before a select audience.

**Recondite:** Obscure: abstruse. From a Latin word meaning *hidden*.

**Reductio ad absurdum:** A method of proving a mathematical proposition by indirection. The Latin expression means *reducing to an absurdity*.

**Redundancy:** Superfluity: excess. From a Latin word meaning *overflowing*.

**Regicide:** One who kills a king: the act of killing a king. From two Latin words meaning *killing a king*.

**Repudiate:** Reject: disown. From a Latin word meaning *to reject*.

**Resilience:** The act or condition of rebounding: elasticity: buoyancy. From two Latin words meaning *to spring back*.

**Rhapsody:** A recitation of an epic passage or a song. From two Greek words meaning *stitching a song*.

**Rival of Thucydides:** This description was applied by the Roman historian Velleius Paterculus to Sallust, Roman historian of the first century B.C.

**Romance languages:** So called because they stem from the Roman or Latin tongue as spoken by garrison soldiers, traders, and similar types. These Romance languages are: Italian, French, Spanish, Portuguese, Rumanian, Provençal: together with such dialects as Romansch, spoken in Switzerland, Corsican, and Sardinian.

**Rome:** Etymologically, Rome means *the town by the Tiber*. Rumon was the old name of the river Tiber.

**Rostrum:** A speaker's platform. Among the Romans, the rostra was a platform, adorned with the beaks (rostra) of captured ships, from which orators addressed the populace.

**Rubicon:** 'To cross the Rubicon' means to take an irretrievable step. In 49 B.C., Julius Caesar, with his armed forces, crossed this stream, which separated Italy from his Gallic province. This act was tantamount to a declaration of Civil War.

# S

**Sacred animals:** Various animals, reptiles, and birds were sacred to certain Greek and Roman divinities. The following associations are of major literary and mythological interest:

Eagle: the bird of Zeus
Peacock: Hera: among the Romans, Juno
Owl: Athena, goddess of wisdom
Wolf: Mars, Romulus
Geese: Juno
Tortoise: Pan
Doves: Venus
Serpent: Aesculapius
Swan: Apollo, Leda
Sparrow: Aphrodite

**Sanctimonious:** Hypocritically professing devoutness or saint-liness. From a Latin word meaning *holy*.

**Sarcophagus:** A tomb. From two Greek words meaning *flesh eating*.

**Satire:** A poem or prose sketch wittily and ironically attacking some individual folly or a social or national vice. From a Latin word meaning *a medley*. In the second century A.D. the Greek Lucian wrote satirical pieces mostly in relation to philosophy, literature, or religion. Juvenal, in the first century A.D., was the most vitriolic satirist among the Romans.

**Saturnalia:** A feast, an orgy, a violent outbreak—as of crime. The Roman festival of the Saturnalia—associated with the old Roman god Saturnus—occurred late in December, and was marked by merrymaking and wild license.

**Saturnine:** Grim, sullen. Astrologically, persons born under the Planet Saturn were believed to be of a gloomy disposition. The word stems from Saturnus, one of the old Roman gods.

**Scene:** A stage setting: the place, circumstances, or surroundings of any occurrence. The term derives from a Greek word meaning *a dressing room* for actors.

**Schism:** A separation, particularly in ecclesiastical matters. From a Greek word meaning *to split*.

**Scholars' Poet:** This designation is applied to Pindar, a Greek lyric poet whose poems are both majestic and obscure.

**Scholia:** Explanatory notes, annotations, written on ancient manuscripts by scholars in the later Roman Empire and in the Middle Ages. From a Greek word meaning *a school, a lecture*.

**Scurrilous:** Abusive: vile. From a Latin word meaning *a jester*.

**Scylla and Charybdis:** 'To be between Scylla and Charybdis' means to be in a dilemma. Scylla and Charybdis were monsters who crushed ships passing through the Straits of Messina.

**Secular:** Relating to the age: concerned with wordly, in contrast to spiritual matters. From a Latin word meaning *an age*.

**Seize the Opportunity:** This gnomic saying—equivalent to the Latin carpe diem—is attributed to Pittacus, one of the Seven Wise Men of Greece.

**Semantics:** The science or study of the meanings of words. From a Greek word meaning *to signify*.

**Seminary:** A training institution: an academy: a place for training ministers of religion. From a Latin word meaning *seed*.

**Sesquipedalian:** Measuring a foot and a half: polysyllabic. From a Latin word meaning *a foot and a half*.

**Seven Wise Men:** A group of seven Greeks of the sixth century B.C. who were noted for their wisdom. These men were: Thales, Cleobulus, Bias, Pittacus, Periandrus, Solon, Chilon. At various periods other names, belonging to other centuries, were substituted in this canon.

**Sibyl:** A priestess-prophetess. The most famous sibyl was the sibyl of Cumae in Italy. In Vergil's Aeneid, she guides the hero through the Lower Regions.

**Siren:** A seductive woman. A siren is also a shrill whistle used as a signal or warning. In Homer's Odyssey, the Sirens were beautiful women who bewitched those who heard their songs.

**Skyscraper:** As early as the third century B.C. there were in Rome apartment houses or flats of three stories. They were called insulae—islands. In Imperial Rome they reached six stories in height.

**Smyrna:** One of the chief claimants to being Homer's birthplace.

**Socratic Irony:** An assumption, on Socrates' part, of mock depreciation, as a humble inquirer who feignedly disparages his own capacities. Socrates, in the Platonic Dialogues, is often accused of this characteristic by his critics. But Socrates himself replies that his only wisdom consists in his awareness of how little he knows.

**Socratic Question:** Since Socrates did not leave any actual writings, how much of the real Socrates is incorporated in the Platonic Dialogues? How much of the historical Socrates is presented by Plato, and to what extent, if any, is Socrates merely a dramatic mouthpiece for Platonic philosophy? This problem, which admits of no finality, constitutes the Socratic Question.

**Sodality:** A fraternity, club, brotherhood. From a Latin word meaning *a friend, crony*.

**Somatic:** Relating to the body: bodily. From a Greek word meaning *the body*.

**Sophistic:** Relating to the Sophists. (See: Sophists.)

**Sophisticated:** Shrewd, worldly-wise. (See: Sophists.)

**Sophists:** The Sophists were Greek philosophers who, as professional teachers, trained men for political, social, and commercial success by means of argumentation whose object was to defeat an opponent without regard to truth.

**Sophrosyne:** Temperateness: prudence: self-control. From two Greek words meaning *whole-mindedness.*

**Soporific:** Inducing sleep. From two Latin words meaning *bringing sleep.*

**Sorites:** A series of syllogisms arranged in propositions so that the predicate of each preceding proposition becomes the subject of the following proposition, the conclusion consisting of the subject of the first proposition with the predicate of the last proposition. This style of sorites is called an Aristotelian sorites, since Aristotle formulated this logical technique. The word sorites itself comes from a Greek word meaning *a heap.*

**Spies:** In Sparta, the secret police who patrolled remote areas and had the authority to kill subversive helots were called Krypteia, the Secret Force.

The Romans too had a spy system that was as sinister and as effective. The head of the Roman Secret Service was the Emperor himself. Spies and informers, delatores, were in his personal pay. These informers acquired tremendous influence with some of the Emperors, and their private wealth increased accordingly. One of their favorite techniques was to have private legacies made invalid so that they would pass to the public treasury, with a consequent bonus to themselves. The practice, begun under Augustus, had by the time of Titus reached such a height of terror, counterplot, and panic that Titus, bent on reform, had spies flogged publicly: then exiled to Sardinia or Corsica, or sold into slavery.

One of the most notorious spies was a certain Regulus. His specialty was informing against innocent persons on charges of treason. The reigns of Nero and of Domitian were his happy hunting-grounds. According to a contemporary, the Younger Pliny, Regulus was a difficult bird to catch. He was rich: he was a shrewd intriguer: he had no small body of followers, and a still larger circle of those who feared him. Regulus, moreover, was a long-winded speaker, always inducing the judges to let him speak on. He had a pleasant little way with him. 'I lost no time,' says Regulus, 'in getting a sight of my opponent's throat, and consider only the easiest way of slitting it.' These tactics, supported by fiendish cold-bloodedness, brought him from utter poverty to immense wealth.

It was unsafe to whisper an innocent remark on last night's gladiatorial show. It was fatal to sit in a tavern with friends and discuss the prospects of the Green and the Blue in the forthcoming chariot races. Even to talk aloud at home was hazardous. Every ear was on the alert. Often the spies resorted to the employment of prostitutes to extract information, reliable or not, from their clients.

Romans, especially those of considerable wealth, lived in continuous dread of the private spy, the blackmailer. Soldiers, dressed as civilians, acted as secret police, frequenting the houses of nobles and inducing frank utterances about the Emperor's person. The informer saw a ready means of financial competence in his grasp, without risk. The only qualification was effrontery. He flourished because executive machinery, responsible for bringing offenders to justice, was rusty and creaking. Any citizen could thus turn informer, bring a criminal action against an innocent citizen, and ruin him. Augustus encouraged the spy system by offering large rewards for convictions of violations of the new marriage laws. The spy was in heaven. Another enactment made disrespectful comment against the Emperor punishable by death and confiscation of property. There were professional 'gangs' to help in this wholesale exile and death of citizens and confiscation of property. Sometimes the Emperor himself, in disguise, would saunter out at night, roaming the city. Sometimes an Emperor would talk in Greek to hide his identity, and listen, in street or tavern, to odd scraps of talk about himself.

Hadrian organized a special corps, the frumentarii, first as police, and subsequently as spies over his own friends.

Tigellinus had Apollonius of Tyana watched constantly, while standing or sitting, speaking or eating. It was noted with whom he ate, when he made sacrifices. Apollonius calls Rome a 'city all eyes and ears.'

Caracalla made the soldiery answerable to him alone for all reports they brought.

In the fourth century Diocletian reorganized the secret police, who persecuted the innocent and concealed crimes such as counterfeiting.

Seneca says all this spying was promoted by the swarms of idlers in Rome. 'Hence this frightful vice of spying on public and private affairs.'

If one melted down an imperial statue, one's property was doomed. A quarter of the estate went to the spy. Under Tiberius, Caligula, Nero, and Domitian, to be denounced by a spy was tantamount to conviction. Two professional spies, Eprius and Cossutianus, accusing the innocent Thrasea and Soranus, were awarded the equivalent of 25,000 dollars each, while an associate, Ostorius, received an amount equal to 6,000 dollars.

On one occasion three Roman senators, bent on a little easy spying, concealed themselves between the roof and the ceiling of a victim's house, while a confederate made the victim talk against the Emperor.

In 24 A.D. a son accused his father, Vibius Serenus, of treason. 'The city was in deep alarm; never was there need of greater caution against a man's nearest relatives. Men were afraid to meet, afraid to talk . . . they even feared things dumb and inanimate, the roofs and the walls.' Thus the historian Tacitus comments on the Roman spy system.

Occasionally, there were respites. At first Caligula made a gesture of discouraging the spies. Nero reduced their personal rewards. Titus repressed them. Domitian checked them at first, then gave them free rain. Spies even crept into Roman prisons, stealthily listening to prisoners' talk. Trajan had all spies banished. They flourished again, however, under Commodus and Caracalla. In the reign of Aurelian, too, political espionage was so rife that victims could not be tried fast enough.

**Squamous:** Scaly. From a Latin word meaning *a scale*.

**Stadium:** An open-air area reserved for athletic and other public performances. Originally, in Greek, the expression meant a course, a race course. At the stadium in Delphi Pythian Games were held every four years in honor of Apollo, who had defeated the monster Pytho.

**Stagirite:** Aristotle is called the Stagirite because he was born in Stagira, in Northern Greece.

**Stenography:** This synonym for shorthand comes from two Greek words meaning *narrow writing*. Tiro, the Greek secretary of Cicero the orator, invented a system of shorthand called Notae Tironianae, the basis of subsequent abbreviated and condensed forms of script.

**Stentorian:** Loud. Stentor was the Greek herald in the Trojan War.

**Stertorous:** Hoarse: deep: heavy. From a Latin word meaning *to snore*.

**Stichomythia:** Dialogue in which each character speaks only one line. From two Greek words meaning *talk in a line of verse*. This type of dialogue is characteristic of ancient Greek drama and of the Roman dramatist Seneca.

**Stigmatize:** To brand: to disgrace. From a Greek word meaning *a mark*.

**Stipend:** Pay: salary. From two Latin words meaning *a gift* and *to pay out.*

**Stoical:** Able to preserve complete indifference to pleasure, pain, or catastrophe. The Stoics were ancient Greek philosophers, followers of their founder Zeno, who taught uncomplaining submission to the vicissitudes of life.

**Stratagem:** A trick: a device: a wile. Originally used in a military sense, but now of general denotation. From a Greek word meaning *a general.*

**Strategy:** The art of generalship. From a Greek word meaning *a general.*

**Strophe:** In Greek dramatic poetry, a lyric stanza.

**Stygian:** Dark. Styx was one of the principal rivers in the Underworld.

**Suasoria:** A rhetorical exercise practiced in ancient Rome, consisting of a subject, usually historical, for a soliloquy.

**Subsidy:** Help: assistance, usually of a monetary nature. From a Latin word meaning *support, reserve,* in a military sense.

**Subterfuge:** An evasion. From two Latin words meaning *fleeing secretly.*

**Summum bonum:** A Latin expression, used in philosophical speculation, meaning *the supreme good:* that is, the ultimate goal in living.

**Sumptuary:** Relating to expenses. In ancient Greece and Rome, as well as in the Middle Ages, sumptuary laws controlled expenditure on clothing, food, and in other directions. From a Latin word meaning *expense.*

**Supercilious:** Disdainful. From two Latin words meaning *raised eyebrows.*

**Supernumerary:** Beyond the number: extra: additional: especially an actor taking part in a crowd scene. From two Latin words meaning *beyond the number.*

**Supplication:** The act of entreating: usually in a religious sense. From a Latin word meaning *to bend.*

**Surreptitious:** Stealthy. From two Latin words meaning *to take away by stealth*.

**Sword of Damocles:** The imminence of a catastrophe. Damocles, envying wealthy Dionysius, was invited to a banquet at which Dionysius placed over his guest's head a sword hanging by a thread. Damocles, disillusioned, realized the evanescent character of luxury.

**Sybarite:** A lover of luxury, a voluptuary. The inhabitants of the Greek city of Sybaris, in Italy, were notorious for their lavish manner of living.

**Sycophant:** A flatterer, a parasite. From two Greek words meaning *a person who shows figs*. One explanation refers to men who informed when figs were stolen from the sacred groves.

**Syllogism:** A technique designed by Aristotle to formulate the process of true reasoning. The syllogism, involving deductive reasoning, consists of three steps, called respectively the major premiss, the minor premiss, and the conclusion. An example of a syllogism is as follows:

> All men are mortal.
> Demetrius is a man.
> Therefore Demetrius is mortal.

**Symposium:** Among the Greeks, a banquet at which there was intellectual or literary discussion. Now, a conference of any kind. From two Greek words meaning *drinking together*. In the third century A.D. Athenaeus produced an encyclopedic Banquet of the Philosophers that is a symposium in the Greek sense.

**Synchronous:** Simultaneous: concurrent. From two Greek words meaning *time together*.

**Syngraphe:** A Greek word applied by the historian Thucydides to his own Peloponnesian War. The word means *a written composition*.

**Synod:** A council: an assembly, particularly of an ecclesiastical nature. From a Greek word meaning *a meeting*.

**Synthesis:** A combination, a merging. From two Greek words meaning *placing together*.

**Syrinx:** A reed pipe. In Greek mythology, Syrinx was a nymph who, to escape the attentions of Pan, was changed into reeds.

# T

**Tachygraphy:** Speedwriting: shorthand. From two Greek words meaning *rapid writing*.

**Taciturn:** Prone to silence: reserved in speech. From a Latin word meaning *silent*.

**Tantalize:** To tease, provoke. In Greek mythology, Tantalus, having betrayed a secret of the gods, was punished by having food and drink set before him, but always beyond his reach.

**Tantalus:** A tantalus is a stand furnished with decanters for holding wine. The word stems from Tantalus. (See: Tantalize.)

**Tartarus:** In ancient mythology, Tartarus was the place of punishment in the Lower Regions. Sometimes Tartarus is synonymous with Hades itself.

**Tautology:** A needless repetition. From Greek words meaning *the same words*. (See: Redundancy: Pleonasm.)

**Technical:** Relating to the mechanical arts: specialized. From a Greek word meaning *an art*.

**Teleology:** The concept that assumes life to have a final design or purpose. From two Greek words meaning *a study of the end* or *issue*.

**Tenderest of Roman Poets:** This description is applied by Tennyson to Catullus, the Roman first century B.C. lyric poet.

**Tenth Muse:** A name applied to the poetess Sappho.

**Ten Thousand:** Ten thousand Greek mercenaries, after fighting for the Persian King Cyrus, were stranded in Asia. But, under the leadership of Xenophon, they finally reached the sea, and their course homeward was clear. This March of the Ten Thousand is described in Xenophon's Anabasis.

**Tergiversation:** Desertion. From two Latin words meaning *turning the back.*

**Terpsichorean:** Relating to dancing. In Greek mythology, Terpsichore was the Muse who presided over dancing.

**Tessellated:** Adorned with a mosaic design. From a Latin word meaning *little cubes.*

**Tetractys of the Decad:** In Pythagorean philosophy, an arrangement of the component parts of the number ten by dots forming a pyramid. This numerical scheme was sacred among the Pythagoreans, and was used in oaths.

**Tetralogy:** In Greek drama, a group of four plays, three of which—the trilogy—dealt with one unified theme. The fourth play, of a lighter type, and involving the god Dionysus, was called a satyr play. The tetralogy was characteristic of Greek dramatic performances. Tetralogy stems from two Greek words meaning *four speeches* or *discourses.* Thematically, the Platonic dialogues are arranged in tetralogies.

**Thalassocracy:** Sea power: rule of the sea. From two Greek words meaning *ruling the sea.* The sea power of Crete in the Minoan Age is a landmark in early Greek history.

**Thales:** Thales of Miletus is considered the first of the Greek 'physiologists' or investigators of natural philosophy. One of his sayings, 'The magnet has a soul because it moves iron,' makes him the virtual founder of magnetism.

**Thanatophobia:** Fear of death. From two Greek words meaning *fear of death.*

**Thaumaturgy:** Magic: witchcraft: the art of performing wonderful feats. From two Greek words meaning *working wonders.*

**Theme:** A topic: the subject of a composition or speech. From a Greek word meaning *setting down, placing*.

**Theogony:** The study of the genealogy of the gods. From two Greek words meaning *birth of the gods*.

**Theophrastus:** A Greek natural scientist of the third century B.C. who produced the first scientific treatise on minerals and gems. He is also considered the Father of Botany.

**Thespian:** Relating to acting, to the drama. As a noun, an actor. Thespis was a Greek dramatic poet of the sixth century B.C., considered the Father of Greek Drama.

**Theurgic:** Relating to divine intrusion in human matters. From two Greek words meaning *work of God*.

**Thrasonical:** Boasting, bragging. From a Greek word meaning *bold*. In "The Eunuch" a comedy by the Roman poet Terence, a character is called Thraso.

**Threnody:** A dirge: a song of lamentation. From two Greek words meaning *a lament* and *song*.

**Timocracy:** Rule by honor. A Platonic state in which love of honor or glory motivates the members. From two Greek words meaning *government by honor*.

**Topography:** The study or description of places. From two Greek words meaning *writing about places*.

**Toxic:** Poisonous. From a Greek word meaning *poison from an arrow*.

**Toxophilite:** A person devoted to archery. From two Greek words meaning *loving a bow*.

**Tradition:** A body of habits and mores transmitted from the past. From two Latin words meaning *handed over*.

**Traduce:** To slander: to defame. From two Latin words meaning *to lead across*.

**Tragedy:** A disastrous situation: a dramatic performance ending in a catastrophe. The word stems from two Greek expressions meaning *a goat song*. In the early religious performances, dedicated to the god of fertility Dionysus, the actors wore goat skins.

**Trilogy:** A series of three dramatic, literary, or musical compositions having some thematic relationship. From two Greek words meaning *three speeches* or *discourses*. In Greek drama, a trilogy was a series of three tragedies with one common motif: for example, Aeschylus' Prometheus Bound, Prometheus Unbound, Prometheus the Fire-Bringer.

**Triptych:** A picture in three contiguous sections: a tablet in three sections. From two Greek words meaning *three fold*.

**Trireme:** A ship equipped with three banks of oars. From two Latin words meaning *three sets of oars*.

**Triton:** In zoology, a marine snail. In ancient mythology, Triton was a minor sea god whose attribute was a trumpet. In his sonnet 'The word is too much with us,' Wordsworth alludes to him:

> I'd rather be
> A Pagan suckled in a creed outworn—
> . . . . .
> Or hear old Triton blow his wreathéd horn.

**Trivium:** A Latin word meaning *a group of three*. The trivium embraced three of the seven arts of mediaeval education, and consisted of grammar, logic, and rhetoric. (See: Quadrivium.)

**Troglodyte:** A cave-dweller: a primitive savage. From two Greek words meaning *cave-dweller*.

**Trojan:** 'To fight like a Trojan' means to fight heroically. A reminiscence of the heroism of the Trojans in their ten year conflict with the Greeks. The epic tale is told by Homer in Greek, in the Iliad, and by Vergil, in Latin, in the Aeneid.

**Trojan Horse:** See: Wooden Horse.

**Truculent:** Grim: ferocious. From a Latin word meaning *wild*.

**Tully:** The usual mediaeval designation for Marcus Tullius Cicero, the Roman orator.

**Tyrant:** A ruthless, domineering person who imposes his will on others. Among the Greeks, tyrant merely meant an unconstitutional ruler, who had overthrown the aristocrats and who might be beneficent in his rule.

**Tyro (tiro):** A beginner: a novice: one who is unpracticed. From a Latin word meaning *a recruit.*

# U

**Unity:** According to Aristotelian theory, there is one indispensable unity: the unity of action: that is, a dramatic piece must deal with one action. Other rules were formulated and elaborated by Renaissance scholars.

**Urbane:** Suave: polished. From a Latin word meaning *relating to a city.* The implication was that a person dwelling in a city was consequently civilized, sophisticated.

**Utopia:** An ideally conceived state or place. From two Greek words meaning *no place.* Throughout the ages, imaginative commonwealths, free from disturbances and inequalities, have been envisaged by philosophers and other writers. The first such state is adumbrated in Plato's Republic. Then follow:

St. Augustine's "De Civitate Dei"—The City of God: 5th century A.D.
Sir Thomas More's "Utopia": 1515.
Francis Bacon's "New Atlantis": 1626.
Campanella's "Civitas Solis"—The City of the Sun: 1630.
Hobbes' "Leviathan": 1651.
Bulwer Lytton's "The Coming Race": 1871.
Bellamy's "Looking Backward": 1888.
William Morris' "News from Nowhere": 1891.
W. D. Howell's "A Traveler from Altruria": 1894.

H. G. Wells' "A Modern Utopia": 1905. "The World Set Free": 1914.

Satirically:

Aldous Huxley: "Brave New World": 1932.

George Orwell: "Nineteen Eighty Four": 1949.

# V

**Vade Mecum:** A book of reference or manual. The expression is itself Latin, meaning *come with me*.

**Venal:** Open to bribery: corruptible. From a Latin word meaning *for sale*.

**Venial:** Pardonable: excusable: e.g. a venial fault. From a Latin word meaning *pardon*.

**Veracity:** Truthfulness. From a Latin word meaning *true*.

**Verbatim:** Word for word. From a Latin word meaning *word for word*.

**Verisimilitude:** An appearance of truth or actuality: plausibility. From two Latin words meaning *like the truth*.

**Via Appia:** The Appian Way: so called from Appius Claudius, who in the fourth century B.C. built the first section of the road, from Rome to Capua—a distance of some 130 miles. The Appian Way was the chief highway of ancient Italy, and finally extended as far as Brundisium.

**Vicarious:** Substituted: substitutional. From a Latin word meaning *change*.

**Vicissitude:** Change: alternation. From a Latin word meaning *a turn, a change*.

**Vigil:** A night watch: watchfulness or wakefulness by night. From a Latin word meaning *to be awake*.

**Virtue is its own Reward:** This is one of the tenets of Socratic philosophy.

**Virtue is Knowledge:** A statement that belongs to the philosophical system of Socrates, whose primary aim was a search for moral values.

**Vituperation:** Abuse: censure. From a Latin word meaning *to blame.*

**Volcano:** A mountain that erupts molten rock, steam, and similar material. From Vulcanus, who, in ancient mythology, was the armorer of the gods. A volcanist is a mediaeval name for a blacksmith.

**Voluble:** Talkative: garrulous. From a Latin word meaning *rolling.*

**Volume:** A book. The Latin word volumen means *a roll of parchment* or *papyrus.*

**Vulcanize:** To treat rubber with sulphur, to produce elasticity. In ancient mythology, Vulcan was the god who fashioned the armor and weapons of gods in his forge.

# W

**Wielder of the Stateliest Measure ever Moulded by the Lips of Man:** This description was applied in an Ode by Tennyson to the Roman epic poet Vergil, who perfected the hexameter verse into a harmonious, majestic instrument.

**Wooden Horse:** During the Trojan War the Greeks built a monstrous wooden horse, and, filling it with soldiery, had it dragged into Troy by the Trojans themselves. The Greeks, stealing out of the horse by night, fell on the Trojans and captured Troy. This is the first classical instance of enemy infiltration.

# X

**Xenolith:** A piece of rock embedded in another rock. From two Greek words meaning *strange stone*.

**Xenophanes:** An Ionian Greek who first enunciated the principles of geology.

**Xenophobia:** Hatred of foreigners. From two Greek words meaning *fear of strangers*. The Greeks, who at times displayed a disdainful attitude toward foreigners, designated non-Greeks as 'barbaroi.'

# Y

**Year of Laches:** 399 B.C., the year in which Socrates was put to death by the Athenians on a charge of irreligion.

# Z

**Zephyr:** A slight breeze. The Latin word zephyrus means *the West Wind*.

**Zoilism:** Harsh criticism or detraction. Zoilus was an ancient Greek literary critic, notorious for his bitter and sharp denigration.

**Zoomorphism:** The representation of animal forms in art and ornamentation. From two Greek words meaning *animal shape*.

### BOOKS THAT MAY BE USEFULLY CONSULTED

*A Literary History of Rome in the Silver Age,* J. Wight Duff. T. Fisher Unwin: London, 1927.

*Handbook of Greek Literature,* H. J. Rose. Methuen: London, 1931.

*Oxford Classical Dictionary.* Clarendon Press: Oxford, 1949.

*Smaller Classical Dictionary.* Dutton: New York, 1952.

*The Literary History of Rome.* From the Origins to the Close of the Golden Age. J. Wight Duff. Ernest Benn: London, 1909. Third Edition, 1953.

EDWIN RADFORD, *Unusual Words,* Philosophical Library: New York, 1946.

J. T. SHIPLEY, *Dictionary of Word Origins,* Philosophical Library: New York, 1945.

P. G. WOODCOCK, *Concise Dictionary of Ancient History,* Philosophical Library: New York, 1955.

P. G. WOODCOCK, *Short Dictionary of Mythology,* Philosophical Library: New York, 1953.